WHITEHEAD, PROCESS PHILOSOPHY, AND EDUCATION

SUNY Series in Philosophy
Robert C. Neville, Editor

Whitehead, Process Philosophy, and Education

Robert S. Brumbaugh
DEPARTMENT OF PHILOSOPHY
YALE UNIVERSITY

STATE UNIVERSITY OF NEW YORK PRESS
ALBANY

Published by
State University of New York Press, Albany

© 1982 State University of New York

All rights reserved

Printed in the United States of America

For information, address State University of New York
Press, State University Plaza, Albany, N.Y., 12246

Library of Congress Cataloging in Publication Data

Brumbaugh, Robert Sherrick, 1918-
Whitehead, Process Philosophy, and Education.

(SUNY series in philosophy)
Includes index.
1. Plato. 2. Education—Philosophy.
3. Reality. I. Title. II. Series.
LB85.P7B78   370'.1   81-14329
ISBN 0-87395-574-9   AACR2
ISBN 0-87395-575-7 (pbk.)

10 9 8 7 6 5 4 3 2 1

Contents

CONTENTS

Acknowledgments

In addition to thanks for permissions to reprint material, I would like to make the following acknowledgments. Nathaniel Lawrence and I have written in collaboration and shared ideas about educational theory for over two decades. It would, in fact, be impossible to separate ideas which were originally my own from ideas which are the result of many productive conversations with him during our long association. A conference on Whitehead's philosophy in relation to education, held in 1980 at the Center for Process Studies in Claremont, California, was stimulating and valuable in clarifying and discussing relevant ideas. An invitation to spend a month at the Rockefeller Foundation Study and Conference Center at Bellagio, Italy in 1981 provided leisure that was not only welcome but essential for finally bringing the parts of this study together. As before, I want to acknowledge my wife's support, including our discussions of ideas and her comments on points of style.

Introduction

After his retirement from Cambridge, Whitehead came to the United States to work on philosophy and education. He had developed a project, in outline, for revising American educational theory and practice, and in 1925 he offered a brief sketch of what he had in mind (*Science and the Modern World*, Ch. 13, "Requisites for Social Progress"). Earlier, in 1922, he had published a pamphlet, *The Rhythm of Education*, which offered another suggestion. The ideas involved are radical departures from the standard thinking of that date, and of the present, and they are grounded firmly in Whitehead's highly technical speculative philosophy. Unfortunately, Whitehead himself never completed his projected work and left most of its applications to be filled in by later scholars.

On current reexamination, Whitehead's ideas seem to me extremely relevant, and their proper development and appreciation may be critical if we are to have a balanced view of the current stylish return to basics theme of educational discussion. This project is one I have been trying to carry out, both in metaphysics and in education, over a considerable time. A number of my chapters are based on lectures and articles developing partial insights into both education and reality.

By and large, Whitehead's educational ideas were developed early in his career, and marked important stages in the development of his mature philosophy. That philosophy, in turn, with its criticisms of current common sense and philosophy of science had important potential implications for education. It is an obvious but important theme in his writings that if education—or anything else—is to be realistic, it must rest on a correct notion of reality. If Whitehead's

1

philosophy is right, that has not been the case for three hundred years and is not the case now. On the contrary, misguided assumptions about the character of location, space, time, and causality are built into the educational system. However, after he came to the United States Whitehead returned only briefly to the theme of education, in the final chapter of *Science and the Modern World*. For the rest he went on developing his cosmology.

The influence of process metaphysics has been strong in American religion and theology, but not comparably so in aesthetics, social science, or educational theory. My present study started as an extension and application of ideas from Whitehead's work to current education. At first what I intended to do was simply to develop the application of key ideas from Whitehead to the educational field. As I worked on this project, however, I found other ideas in the Platonic tradition that seemed as relevant and helpful as Whitehead's so the scope of the ideas being applied widened. I have finally, I think, worked out my study in the tradition of Platonic metaphysics that includes the new emphasis on the concrete introduced by process thought. In fact, my first chapter examines two insights into reality which have shaped Western education; one of these is a classical formalism, which in an extreme form would be very like the principle of limitation in Plotinus; the other is the principle of plenitude with a return to temporality which would lead to modern Platonisms close to Whitehead's. My final chapter brings together, I think without inconsistency or incongruity, Whitehead's lecture "Immortality" and Plato's *Phaedo*. In between there are discussions of ways in which education can be brought into better agreement with reality. A natural but still mistaken over-generalization of 17th-century physics, is the main target of proposed revisions.

The next two decades promise to be critical for American education. Not satisfied with the present system, advocates of a return to basics are calling for concentration on language skills and computation. I think that this is a misunderstanding of the options that are realistic and open, and would make the situation worse.

Whitehead diagnosed some of the causes for our dissatisfaction with current education, and with ourselves, correctly. One of his insights

2

was that both our common sense and our social science have over-generalized the ideas of 17th-century physics. Those ideas were a highly selective set of abstractions, focusing on only those properties relevant to inanimate material particles moving and colliding. The elegance and success of these explanatory ideas of *physics* led to their being transformed into principles of *metaphysics*, which is quite another thing. This transformation takes the concepts of physics to be the description of the whole of reality. Following from this, of course, came a new criterion for judging what is realistic in education and social planning. If, as is the case when this extension is made, our view of reality is one-sided and ill-considered, so will our social systems be.

A case in point that Whitehead discussed is the acceptance of the technical notion that space functions only as an insulator. For small material particles, it is useful to assume that any two do not influence each other unless there is some kind of contact. But when we generalize this notion of all kinds of things and all kinds of spaces, the result is clearly mistaken. In the interests of a supposed "realism," we can treat every nation as a unit radically insulated—except for contact along frontiers—from every other. The result is irrational nationalism and imperialism. We apply the model to individuals in society, and the result is irresponsible egoism. We extend it to cosmology, and the result is a materialism that seems to make any reconciliation of reality and religion an impossibility.

When we correct this view by using a notion of location that comes closer to fitting our own actual psychological and social experiences, it turns out, for example, that persons are not isolated in the way solid particles seem to be. The identity of each of us extends over and includes the culture, society, and civilization that we participate in. There is no isolated, solitary self imprisoned in its own body. In an obvious and convincing aside, Whitehead, remarking on the fact that people interact at a distance through social space, says that every hostess recognizes this as she plans a dinner party.

This suggests a first aim for education. We must stop thinking about learning and teaching with models that identify students with stupid particles and classroom space with an insulating vacuum. We must consider the content we are teaching as well, so that we do not indoctrinate our students with a misguided savage individualism that the mistaking of classical physics for metaphysics made us believe to be realisitic.

Further corrections and improvements are in order as well. Two of the most important were also suggested by Whitehead as implications of process philosophy; but he did not develop the suggestions in full detail. The first suggestion is that education should pay more attention to the appreciation of concrete things. Since classical times, we have accepted a biased and exclusive rationalism in our curricular designs. Following the slogan that the aim—the sole aim—of education is to train the intellect, we have concentrated exclusively on facility with abstractions—numbers, names, mental discipline. That discipline is, in fact, essential. But it is easy to forget that general terms gain their efficiency by leaving everything non-essential to their functioning out of account. The kind of quick recognition-in-outline that goes with classifying and naming is at exactly the opposite pole from the unique appreciation that gives an aesthetic quality to concrete encounter. In a world that contains unique individuals, which nevertheless sort out well into kinds and types, pretending that the only real or really important entities are disembodied networks of abstractions misses all aesthetic experience. The correction, as Whitehead suggested, is to make concrete appreciation as important an aim of education as we now make intellectual discipline.

The point at which process philosophy and current educational proposals collide head-on, however, is not so much over the issues we have mentioned, space and concreteness, but rather over the relation of learning and time. Existence in time, according to process metaphysics, is dynamic, directed, irreversible, and taking place in successive phases. For very small, particle-sized events, these "phases of concrescence" constitute the life of each event; and they must occur in fixed order. There is an initial encounter of some kind; a phase of readjustment which is unstable; and a final stabilization that marks the end of that event. For more complex entities, including persons and civilizations, an analogous rule holds. If learning is to be an integral part of a student's existence and growth, it must follow the three-stage pattern in which growth and concrescence take place. Whitehead's stages of learning are romance, precision, and generalization or satisfaction. A student, however, unlike the minimal event, is a complex entity which will continue to exist—though less authentically and effectively—even if he or she does not encounter proper learning patterns. But a pattern that fails to match the natural stages of process frustrates life and learning—it is disregarded, accommodated to as an external accident, passed by with no important—or even unimportant—gain in insight or in depth.

The metaphysical point is that all actualization, from particles through persons to civilizations and evolutionary epochs, must be achieved in an irreversible sequence of phases. For learning, the first stage of this sequence must be the one of romance—strong motivation to explore a field or collection seen as extending to the horizon, but not yet surveyed and articulated into disciplined detail nor enclosed by a general architectonic frame.

To omit this stage and begin instead with discipline and precision has been a constant temptation since classical times and earlier. It is, of course, what our contemporary back to basics movement advocates. And it is certain to fail. Interest is killed off, subject-matter is made dull, motivation can only be extrinsic (introducing a kind of ethical mis-education), and the lesson forgotten as soon as it is over. Or, if not forgotten, rote material is retained unreflectively as pebble-like bits of information at the price of continual rote review. (The classical one-sided emphasis on abstraction offered a similar temptation. Since its aim was, generally speaking, appreciation of form—literary, mathematical, dialectical—particular content seemed irrelevant. Why Sophocles rather than Shakespeare? And noting this, educators attempted—particularly clearly, in the case of syllogistic logic—to teach the forms without any distracting content at all. There is nothing more vacuous and deadly; and the logic of syllogism never gained a deserved popularity that could have spared us dangerous short circuits in our forms of thought.)

I continue my discussion through two more topics. The first is the need to reinterpret our notion of causality. This idea was, like that of space, a metaphysical generalization from the physics of the 17th century. Without being aware of it, we accept systems of formal logic, of mathematics, of theoretical physics that presuppose an identical quality for past, present, and future time. How this relates to our notions of human responsibility, freedom, and creativity is left unexamined, perhaps lost somewhere in a corridor between the physics and the civics classrooms; but it need not be. Some simple modifications of logic that take account of time modalities and tenses can offer more flexible formal systems more closely matching a world where time is dynamic and actual, not abstract and empty.[1]

Finally, an educational curriculum and theory which is truly realistic must end in and include a vision of our place and our importance in cosmology. The Platonic tradition, including but at some points reaching beyond process philosophy, provides such a cosmic vision of human *collective* and *individual* importance and immortality. It also offers a way of understanding, and of modifying, the apparent contradictions of responsible scientific certainty and intuitively irresistible religious vision. My final suggestion is not a recommendation of religious education, but of appreciation of cosmology for showing us the great patterns of process and reality, and our place in them.

CHAPTER ONE

Education and Reality: Two Revolutions

In 1971, I was invited to give the annual Suárez lecture on metaphysics by the Fordham University Department of Philosophy. The reason, I was told, was that the students in the department wanted an approach that would be "relevant" and the faculty hoped my interest in education might qualify me for the assignment. Thus the invitation was less of an endorsement of my expertise as a metaphysician than I might have wished, and much more of a challenge to combine the themes of education and reality. The successive discoveries and the proper relation of the two great metaphysical principles of limitation and plenitude seemed to be a theme that would meet the challenge. For the present book, the Fordham lecture seems to me a good opening chapter, indicating the connection of the first section, on "Reality" and the second, on "Education." It sets up the general frame within which an exploration of concreteness will illuminate the theme of plenitude, discipline that of limitation, and philosophic vision that of their proper combination.

We need a total revolution in educational theory, and there are good metaphysical reasons why this is so. Yet we cannot hope for chance miraculously to supply something better if we simply dissolve the present system and have no other structure on hand to replace it; there are excellent metaphysical reasons for that, too. In all this busy revolt and reconstruction, we are told that we need to be aware of the implications for education of new findings in technology, psychology,

Reprinted by permission of the publisher from *Thought*, vol. 48, no. 188 (Spring 1973) (New York: Fordham University Press, 1973), copyright © 1973 by Fordham University Press, pp. 5–18.

and anthropology; for this there may also be good reasons, but they are contingent and empirical. Still, I will begin with this last theme.

From time to time, I write on 3x5 cards items which I think will interest my periodic philosophy of education seminars. By and large, I refer to these items to pose questions that I hope my students will answer or at least remember. The first card in the stack now on my desk cites the issue of *Life* magazine with the caption "EVE WAS FRAMED" on the cover, stating the case for women's liberation. Obviously, our schools have done a great job of institutionalizing the myths of female difference and inequality. It is equally obvious that the process should be reversed. But how do we set about it? One thinks at once of many item-by-item changes in tactics: we might have boys take cooking and girls take shop (that was actually tried forty-five years ago in the school I went to); we might insist that guidance counselors press for careers in science for talented girls; we might put more about great women into our history books. But my experience convinces me that none of these will do much good if, in the background, a fundamental presupposition remains that women are, and should be kept, inferior. Because it takes philosophy to recognize such overarching unexpressed presuppositions, we need educational philosophy as well as educational technology. (At some point, though, we do need the technology as well.)

My second 3x5 card cites an advertisement for a new, cheap desk calculator in *Scientific American*. As the downward trend in calculator cost continues, we will soon be able to give up the teaching of computation five days a week for ten years, with its constant pattern repetition varied only by new and ugly intransigent figures. Since medieval times,[1] new techniques have transformed long division from black magic to routine; why not carry this change one step further? The cash register and desk calculator, supplemented by a purse-size adder or slide rule, can do the calculations without spending ten years learning routines in elementary school.

My third card turns out not to be a current citation, but a reference to a new idea of "aesthetic interest" in one of Whitehead's essays, published in 1918, and never reprinted since (*The Organization of Thought*, Ch. III). In that essay, he argued that appreciation as well as abstraction must be developed by education and that there is no reason

8

why "aesthetic appreciation" must be limited to the traditional works and canons of "fine art."

Other cards have references to such things as an article on transfer of information from short-to-long-term memory; a book called *Working Models of Ancient Machines* (misleadingly subtitled "Easily Built by the Reader"); a logic with tenses—a project which I recommended several years ago in my Presidential Address to The Metaphysical Society of America. Going on two cards more, the next card refers to board games and their rather stark simulations of modern times (in particular, a pair called "Careers" and "Operation"), and the second card refers to archaeological evidence for the invention of the wheel (apparently the work of ancient proto-Siberians).

The trouble with this 3x5 card approach is that we are dealing with educational and intellectual systems, and not with isolated items. When one pulls out a small piece of information and tries to press another into the empty space, the new piece gets squeezed down and reshaped by the structural steel framework so that it fits in, leaving the Eiffel Tower structure just as it was before. Cooking classes for boys have no automatic implications for feminine equality—indeed, as early as Plato (*Republic* V) we find male cooks asserting a chauvinistic superiority. Mathematics, even after the demise of long division, can still become rote work with an arcane terminology of set theory. Even a "new aesthetic" outlook in art can merely lead to a few new things in old frames in familiar galleries—a snow-shovel, a colored transparency of an oil refinery.

The only hope for progress when one must change a system is in a systematic change; and the only way to plan that kind of change is philosophically, for it is only with philosophy that one can recognize the framework of presuppositions in the higher levels of generality of the system, and judge their adequacy by the degree to which they are realistic. Such a judgment must combine philosophical analysis and metaphysical speculation, since to determine what is or is not realistic requires a prior knowledge of what is real.

So I have been forced to go beyond my 3x5 cards and try an experiment in metaphysics, properly applied. Obviously, I have been using my card file as a symbol for the totality of narrowly focused techniques, proposals, and dissents of current educational journals and literature. To go beyond this and attempt to bring together some of the abstract subtlety of Suárez and some of the immediacy of Holt or Leonard or Herndon is not easy. Yet this is what I am going to do, because after watching almost a half century of tinkering with educational technology my conclusion—pessimistic or not—is that the revolution which we need cannot be effected in any less ambitious way.

There have been only two great revolutions in Western educational thought, each coinciding with a new recognition of an important metaphysical principle. The scene of the first was ancient Greece at the turn of the fourth century B.C.; and we ourselves are living in the second. The Greek revolution, a discovery of the power of reason and the importance of form, was a part of the recognition of the metaphysical principle of limitation. To be is to be something; and to be something is to have defining properties that constitute an identity, and locate an individual within a kind or type. Types and kinds, in turn, exist in hierarchies so ordered that belonging to a general type is a necessary condition for fitting into a specific one. As the Greeks discovered, the logical relations among the forms in these hierarchies reappear as causal laws and temporal relations among their instances. Recognition of a thing's form thus turns out to be a key to prediction, planning, and teaching, as well as simply classification, a key which goes far beyond Mycenean funded experience innocent of logic or generalization. The Greek discovery of form, and of human ability to recognize it, was both revolutionary and, in its historic context, realistic. And it dominated Western educational thought—as an exclusive aim implicit in the background—until the present century.

But there is a second, equally important, metaphysical principle which the Greeks tended to take for granted and later Western cultures tended to mention in theory but ignore in practice. This is the principle of plenitude: a recognition that concrete individuals are more than mere type-outlines in space and time, infinitely more, and that this greater complexity gives them an added dimension of aesthetic interest. If you take away its triangularity, no plane figure can be a triangle. But unless you add definite size and angles pure triangularity cannot be realized in any concrete situation. And when it is realized, any concrete triangle will have infinitely more properties than necessarily follow from its abstract definition.

Our current revolution rests, ultimately, on the correct recognition that this principle of plenitude is just as real and as important as the classical principle of limitation. From this perspective, it seems that the whole Western ideal of education has crystallized into a system that is one-sided in its emphasis on abstractions and its tendency to equate logical sequences with genetic ones. We are so familiar with *form* that it is hard for us to appreciate the Greek educational enthusiasm for "liberal arts" that stressed appreciation of general patterns, types, and laws. It is only if we look back at the debate over education in Socrates' time, and consider what might have happened if history had decided in another way, that we begin to appreciate the importance—and the good luck for us—of the fact that Socrates, Plato, and Aristotle won. It was a three-way discussion.

There were conservative advocates of an educational system which stressed a mixture of Homer and practical conditioning, holding fast to ideas that were formed in an age of chivalry three centuries before. So far as funded information and technique are concerned, this emphasis on Homeric epic was not as perverse as it sounds to us today; for in fact, one function of the oral tradition as we find it in Homer was to provide a kind of reference encyclopedia, a story account of each ritual and taxonomy. At the same time, the user of this treasury was invited to accept it uncritically, although it offered neither causal explanation, general law, nor challenge to inquiry. The role of Homer has sometimes been compared to the role that the Bible has played in some fundamentalist Christian communities.

The main trouble with this conservative educational tradition was that it had become hopelessly out of date. The Neo-Mycenean idea of a life aimed at glory in the eyes of society had been modified by the discovery of the individual; the notions of commerce as either barter or piracy had little to do with the operations of the Athenian agora; the older idea of a gentleman was a stereotype too illiterate and savage to fit the urban scene. Nevertheless, there were conservatives—the comic poet Aristophanes among them—who wanted no innovation.

Ordinarily, I would not digress to speculate on the metaphysical presuppositions of the Homeric tradition and the bardic mind. But on this occasion it seems worth doing for a moment. If Snell is at all right, or Havelock, or Cassirer, or any of a number of other scholars, the concept of reality presupposed by the Homeric epic is radically fragmented and paratactic. Time comes in days; personal identity dissolves into a loose conjunction of limbs, impulses, and livers; nature is run by idiosyncratic local deities; space is mythical rather than mathematical. (I think it fair to say that no medieval scholar, nor any modern one until our own century, really re-created this world of Homer in its full impersonal vanity, transient disorder, and cyclic triviality.) In short, insofar as there was any anticipation of metaphysics, there was, perhaps, some plenitude—though the stereotyped language, characterization, and plot make one wonder even about that—with no significant recognition of limitation.

The second option for education was suggested by the Sophists. Professional teachers of success, with no great patience for antiquated standards, they were indeed an antithesis to the earlier submergence of the individual in the community and culture. Education, as they saw it, should consist of techniques, skills, and bits of cultural information that help one get ahead: rhetoric, law, etiquette. Where the naive traditionalist assumed that there is a human nature everywhere identical with the customs of his own local province, the Sophists assumed that all values—except individual greed for pleasure and power—existed only "by convention." They were not much interested in scientific or philosophical generalization: we have various records of their criticisms of the uselessness of mathematics and natural philosophy. Nor were they very curious about the nature of a self: for their learning theory, they used the model of a machine that stored and retrieved information, while for their ethics they used a model that reminds me a bit of current work on intra-specific aggression and operant conditioning. Perhaps the magnificent Hippias, inventor of the reference book, the art of mnemonics, and the quiz program, is a fitting apotheosis of this conception of what education might be: skill, information, conditioned conformity. And—if we can trust the portraits of him left by the Academy—a total inability to grasp inductive generalization.

Once again, a look at an implicit metaphysics may be in order. What we find this time is in fact a humanistic variation on the atomic theory. The elements are real, their compounds derivative or arbitrary. The Sophists and atomists are often associated on the basis of the

12

opposition of nature to convention in the fragments of Democritus. That seems to me less relevant than their common use of atomistic, mechanistic models. There is no room in such models for freedom or dignity; no guarantee of any conservation save of matter and momentum; no creativity, but mere recombination; and no subject worth mentioning, but an isolated, egoistic center of appetite.

The third tradition, that of liberal education, began with the discoveries of pure mathematics and physical science in the sixth century B.C. Very quickly, the ideas appeared that there are explanations which are naturalistic rather than mythological; that there are laws of nature; and that those laws are fundamentally mathematical. But for some time this "scientific" tradition concentrated its attention on cosmology: it assumed that the scientist could somehow stand outside of the world he was describing, like a god in epic poetry. It was only with Socrates' question as to the nature of a human self that the full range of questions formalism must answer became clear. But after that question, from Socrates through Plato and Aristotle, the conviction was shared that the aim of education is the kind of freedom that comes from understanding general principles, causes, and sequences. The paratactic epic world was replaced by a tidy reasoned system in which there is tight logical and causal order, and whose universal laws make accurate prediction possible.

The appreciation of form came to dominate this tradition of classical thought. There are forms of thought, which enable us to reason logically and to construct systems that are true. There are forms of legality and social order which enable us to build ethical systems that protect the essential equality of all fellow citizens. There are forms of closure, sequence, and symmetry which seem to the classical critic and artist the necessary conditions for realization of beauty.

At the same time that these universal formal patterns structure logic, ethics, and aesthetics, the forms have three epistemological functions. They are the common meanings that make language possible; they are the types and structures that descriptive science looks toward; and they are the ideals or goals that serve as criteria in ethics and aesthetics. In order to play these parts, it seemed clear to the classical thinkers that the theory of forms would not work unless it had some cooperation from reality. And down to the present time there have been Platonists who reaffirm this view. Writing in defense of Platonism in mathematics, Prof. René Thom says:

> Everything considered, mathematicians should have the courage of their most profound convictions and thus affirm that mathematical forms indeed have an existence that is independent of the mind considering them. This existence is without doubt different from the concrete existence of the external world, but it is still subtly and deeply related to it. If mathematics is only an arbitrary game which is the random product of cerebral activity, how can one explain its unquestioned success in describing the universe? Mathematics is found not only in the mysterious fixed order of physical laws, but also, in a more hidden though equally certain manner, in the infinite succession of animate and inanimate forms and in the formation and breaking up of their symmetries. Despite appearance, this is why the hypothesis stating that Platonic ideas give shape to the universe is the most natural, and, philosophically, the most economical.[2]

And, within limits—though less exactly than Greek enthusiasts assumed after rounding off—the method of generalization does in fact enable us to predict, to explain, and to classify. The power of the multiplication table, or the chemical periodic table, or the law of freely falling bodies, does not rest on its aesthetic appeal: the limitations are objectively there. On this point, Plato and Aristotle agreed; and on the further point, that freedom requires self-knowledge in addition to knowledge of the laws of nature, they agreed as well. It was this third point of view, that education should capitalize on our powers of abstraction and generalization, which finally won out in the ancient debate over the aims of education. If it had not, we might have waited a long time, or forever, for science; for intellectual curiosity; for a concept of justice that embodied the principle of legality; for an efficient medical or industrial technology. In fact, of the three competing notions, education as mere phantasy, or simple technology, or understanding, it was the third which was the most realistic. Being in tune with the cosmic principle of limitation, its merits were recognized and liberal education became our Western ideal.

Unfortunately, the victory was something of an overkill. The rationalists countered Sophistic proposals that education replace useless studies with weaving or carpentry, with their own ill-natured diatribes against menial and slavish crafts, diatribes which came to be misunderstood when the proposals they countered had been forgotten—and they were certainly forgotten by the second century A.D. The stress on temperance and moderation, as these virtues were construed in a Greek city state, transmuted into something devoid of feeling and color when the words stayed the same but the world depersonalized and took on sharp corners in the era of the Roman Empire. The power given by a grasp of the forms of things suggested an unholy educational shortcut: teaching only the forms, while forgetting the things entirely. The liberal arts experimented for centuries with this shortcut of grasp-of-form-without-content. If this were possible, we would be living in a very different universe from the one we do in fact inhabit! Yet it seems true that if there were not a principle of limitation, we could not envisage or define the true, the right, or the good; we would only constantly encounter novelties categorizable as "interesting." And that thought tempts me to digress from Western theory, for a moment, to cite an insight from the Far East: there is a Chinese curse, "May you live in an *interesting* time."

It is the principle of plenitude that accounts for this curse, or blessing, of interest. That principle establishes the relevance of forms to instances: the form sets the limits within which an instance must remain, on pain of losing any title to the form at all. A square that decides to become round ceases to be a square; it does not become a round square. The limitations are sharp, and they are brittle. But there are an infinite number of properties which are logically irrelevant to the instance of a form, yet existentially essential. This sounds overly metaphysical, but perhaps it will make more sense with an example.

Robert Hartman, in his work on formal value theory, uses the example of a girl to show the difference between the values of mere membership in a class, a type specimen, and a fully existent unique individual. For purposes of a man tallying the sex and number of pedestrians passing Sullivan's Bar, the girl exists only on the highest level of abstraction. He notices—at least in this role of taxonomist he need notice—only two defining properties: an abstract outline that is human and feminine which he records by a mark in column F. But, of course, there is no such thing as a female human being in the abstract: it may be logically irrelevant, but to be a girl does existentially involve being a certain size, with a definite eye color, height, and so on. And as the girl goes beyond Sullivan's Bar to the Park Street corner, the young men there look at her as a typical girl. That is, they imagine taking her to a dance or a football game, having a conversation, going to a movie. She is much more interesting as a type than as a mere tally, representing what Hartman calls an explication of a concept rather than a mere definition. She is the kind of girl that probably would (or would not) be my type. But notice that the type is still something of an abstraction: within the limits it respects, there still is room for individuality. In addition to being a tall, blue-eyed, well-coordinated sort of person, this girl is an individual who has her own unique biography, style, and ideas. And this individuality is the only way in which a type can take on concrete existence and value. The boy she is on her way to meet will see the girl in this third role.

Twentieth-century Platonism—Whitehead's in cosmology, Hartman's, perhaps, in value theory, various formalists in logic—goes back for a second look at the principle of plenitude. For, while having a form is a necessary condition for being a type specimen, it is not sufficient; nor is being a typical example a sufficient condition for being a concrete individual instance. Two of Whitehead's conclusions about education nicely reflect this Platonic second look. His first conclusion is that education should give equal weight to facility with abstractions and to appreciation of concrete persons, things, and situations. Words and numbers are the tools of abstract thought; but when we make them the entire content of education, the process and product have become one-sided and any sense of wonder or value is bleached out of the student's world. The past assumptions may have been that everyone automatically has concrete appreciation; that it is no trick at all to apply abstract ideas, once we get them clear; that in fact wonder and vividness are usually tempting distractions, interfering with education. But if so, past assumptions were mistaken—even though the mistakes were perpetuated for two thousand years. Whitehead's second conclusion is that learning cannot effectively start without some desire to learn on the part of the student. Learning is a three-phase affair, moving from a stage of romance to one of precision to one of generalization or satisfaction. To start with the intellectual discipline which is the abstract precision of a subject matter—or a craft—will kill off interest and require vigorous extrinsic reinforcement if work is to go on. This is in line with our earlier observation that attempts to shortcut the teaching of the appreciation of form by presenting pure form devoid of any content have always failed. For in effect the abstract taxonomy of Greek nouns or of inorganic chemicals is interesting just insofar as some concrete use and context makes them so.

Throughout twentieth-century culture—perhaps most clearly in our writings on education, but in many other places as well—the rediscovery of the principle of plenitude is being celebrated. The first temptation, of course, is to reject, insult, and minimize the principle of limitation which had been responsible, it is felt, for unrealistic neglect of the concrete and the individual. There is a glorification either of action or of appreciation at the expense of thought. And there is a claustrophobic reaction to constraining form: of the school building, the city, the subway, the conventions of middle-class culture.

It is not surprising that this should happen; for a new metaphysical insight, genuinely felt, is an intoxicating thing. And this trend does reflect a new dimension in our vision of what is real and what is important. I do not mean to say that Western philosophers and educators would ever have just flatly denied the principle of plenitude; indeed, even Plotinus recognizes it in the *Third Ennead*. But they did not believe it enough to try it operationally, to introduce a symmetry into the treatment of abstraction and concrete instantiation and change the aims, materials, and methods of life and education.

In the light of this great interest, and of what I have said about its metaphysical causes, I would be inconsistent if I were now to end with a detailed prescription for our current revolution. Clearly, there are many ways in which students can learn, many ways in which truths and skills can be taught. On the other hand, there are certain limits and directions that are relevant to what is going on. For example, I would assume that even on the level of an elementary school, we would want the pupils to have some first-hand contact both with forms that set limits and concrete situations that operate within those limits in creative and interesting ways.

For purposes of symmetry and completeness, I would like to return to the world of technology and detail where we began—my boxes of 3x5 cards—and at least indicate some areas that I think must be included in any constructive planning of schools and curricula. However, this is a postscript to my principal theme; and I make it brief, hoping not to distract attention from the main ideas it illustrates.

In whatever way it is done, we must have work in ecology—both theory and practice—to give our students some awareness of their place in nature and their responsibility for the environment. I like the notion of practical ecology; for years, educators have been trying to find projects that would permit younger members of the community to make some shared contribution to it and this provides a way. I am, you see, beginning to set up a new order and put new labels on my boxes of 3x5 cards. If I arrange these boxes from plenitude to limitation, reading from left to right, the ECOLOGY box goes toward the left.

Far to the right of my new filing scheme will be a new box for ideas dealing with logical form. It is time that we actually used the insights available since the Greeks into the principle of limitation as it relates to reasoning. Thee is no more excuse for confusing sound patterns of thought with their unsound cousins than there is for confusing mushrooms with toadstools. The results are sometimes just as lethal in the former case as in the latter. But logic as it is usually taught concentrates so hard on the limitation principle that plenitude is lost, and with it interest and applicability. There is nothing harder for a lecturer on logic to do than to reverse his attention from pure pattern to impure application, and to come up with an example. Aristotle, for instance, seems to have stared at a painting of Socrates in the back of his lecture hall whenever his mind went blank in the search for an illustration, unless he first noticed student Coriscus—musical, pale of complexion—in the front row. For by itself the principle of limitation is lacking in interest and value. It can shrink to an austere rule of formal validity that allows for the consideration of neither probability nor ethical consistency.

A second box lying toward the right of my scheme will have cards dealing with the principle of limitation in its social role—with the concept of persons as sharing legal equality. Formally and logically, the point seems almost trivial: it merely amounts to saying that if something holds for any person, x, then if a and b are particular persons, it holds for a and b. Yet human history is an almost constant record of ways in which priests, kings, wealthy merchants, and male chauvinists have contrived to evade this simple logical substitution principle. Current discussion of integration in relation to school bussing carries on the same attempt to evade logic and justice.

Now, having a storehouse for ideas on ecology as representing plenitude, and logic and legality representing limitation, I immediately need two more categories in between, one for aesthetic sensitivity and one for new school design. Aesthetic sensitivity has to do with that aspect of the principle of limitation which appears as aesthetic compatibility, and with that aspect of the principle of plenitude which appears as creativity. The strange thing about this aspect of reality is that appreciation and sensitivity can be learned, but in no ordinary sense of teaching can they be taught. In our century, and by no means uniquely here, insensitivity and lack of imagination are great sources of lost opportunities—for equality, for fraternity, for better dinner parties. We need to notice people and things as we rush along, each of us on his fenced-in super-highway of efficiency.

And my final box, ideas bearing on new school design, will have a motto: SCHOOL PROBABLY SHOULD BE INEFFICIENT ABOUT HALF THE TIME. I need to keep looking at this as a reminder to keep my sense of humor and be less intense in my mad urge to cover the material; I need to enjoy teaching. The content can begin with a cross-reference card: SEE THE OTHER BOXES MARKED ECOLOGY, LOGIC, ETHICS, AESTHETIC SENSITIVITY. And then, as a second cross-reference: SEE ALSO PHILOSOPHY, SUB-SECTIONS HEADED PLENITUDE AND LIMITATION. This is a nice realistic way to move ahead with our current revolution.

As I began by saying, we need a revolution if we are to achieve a more realistic theory and practice of education—and the examined and satisfying human life which is education's aim. I have been trying to offer some guidelines, or at least a prologue, for that revolution by showing a connection between realistic living and learning, and the nature of reality.

CHAPTER TWO
Space: Neither Void nor Plenum

Historically, process philosophers have been fascinated by time, and rather bored by space. There is a reason for this: spatially oriented models and plans lead naturally to philosophies which spatialize time and change. It is a mistake, however, to overlook the notions of space and location; it is not necessary to leave these concepts to the abstractness of a static formal model, or to unanalyzed technological common sense. In fact, it is necessary not to, if we want to philosophize well. For inattention to spatial concepts may interfere with both the theoretical consistency and the practical efficacy of process philosophy.

Aristotle, an excellent observer, thought that every change of location in terrestrial space took place through a medium that had some resistance. If the space which related places were wholly empty, he thought, it would be pure non-entity, and so unable to have contents or contain relations; while a wholly filled space would be a plenum, an extended substance in its own right, and thus unable to contain or transmit anything else. This Aristotelian empirical notion of a field which is neither vacuum nor plenum seems to me to be right. Interaction must take account not only of intensity and distance, but of the space through which the distance is measured, and its coefficients of conduction and insulation.

Reprinted by permission of the publisher from *Process Studies*, VII (1979): 161–172. Copyright 1979 by the Society for Study of Process Philosophy, Claremont, California.

I

Between the time when Aristotle included the "where" in his categories and the time when Whitehead criticized "simple location," the question of places where things are attracted rather slight attention from philosophy. The tacit assumption was that the physical or metaphysical places in question could be identified with sets of mathematical points, or with knife-edged states, or with quasi-mathematical monads. And Whitehead's reopening of the theme used this concept only in passing, as an arbitrarily chosen case study of the difference between scientific abstractions and adequate common sense. Nevertheless, it was an important case study. It was important because the abstract scientific concept of location that Whitehead found dominant in current common sense led to further notions of inside and outside, here and there, that were inadequate philosophically and inefficient practically.

Whitehead himself, particularly concerned to protect the primary role of time in his physical theories, made space abstract and derivative. By contrast, my discussion centers on space as primary, as a kind of venture in metaphysical topology; the project is Whiteheadian in inception, but my own in execution. I propose to show the inadequacy of two extreme notions of space and place by testing them against our experiences of social space wherein we are the entities contained by the social field. I assume that such social fields are in fact spaces and that the behavior of entities contained in them is relevant to any philosophical theses about location.

II

A *space* is a continuous field made up of distance relations; it can be defined geometrically. Whether the space is something substantial that contains related entities, or whether it is generated by the relations of things does not matter for the present discussion. Space can contain entities; and entities can interact in and through space. This interaction can be thought of apart from dynamic time as forces at a moment, state, or small section. Space is alike in all directions; the entities and relations it contains are all actual; and for distances such as S, $S(x,y)$

always equals $S(y,x)$. Further, an object moved through a space, then returned to its starting point, is not affected by its shifts of position.

Unlike space, *time* is a set of relations of entities which form a sequence. A sequence is not the same in every direction, but has an irreversible temporal direction of its own. The terms are transitively connected, but they are not reversible. Some terms of a sequence are actual (its past), some only potential (its future). The actual terms are entities which are causally connected.

An *actual entity* is a substance located at a point of intersection of a spatial distance scheme and a temporal causal sequence. (Thus the definitions of space and time also specify what sorts of entity the spatio-temporal system can include.) A *process* is a sequence in which a special kind of causality, "creative activity," gives direction to the constituents.

In physical spaces we can disregard temporal effects. There remains, however, interaction along distance lines, or lack of it, which pure mathematical space does not have. And an adequate general characterization of space, able to include natural as well as mathematical types, must accommodate neutral, insulating, and conductive space.

In fact, at the very limits of the natural world, there seem to be perfect conducting and insulating spaces. At the one extreme lies the superconduction of a field at absolute zero temperature; at the other, the lack of radiation in a field of black hole entities with infinite density (so that they no longer mutually exert gravitational influence). By and large, however, the spaces we are interested in are normal in the sense that they fall somewhere between the infinitely full and infinitely empty.

III

A first experiment with a concept of space follows a suggestion of Whitehead's. He pointed out that the idea that physical things are each simply located in a Cartesian pure space is a case of a past technical concept diffused into present common sense (SMW, Ch. 3). What happened seems to have been that the past technical notion of location from Cartesian physics was made into a metaphysical notion of location generally, and uncritically accepted. Whitehead described this differently, saying that current common sense was the heir of past metaphysics. But in the present case, what we have seems rather to be a current common sense (and metaphysics) resulting from generalization of past technical science.

In this current version, all spaces are presupposed to be perfect insulators. Thus, two things in distinct places are totally irrelevant to each other, unless those places are in immediate or mediated contact. For some purposes, this conception of things, each in its proper place, will work quite well: it seems quite congenial in the context of mechanics, invention, and technology. But in other contexts it runs into difficulties, both theoretical and practical. A case of a practical problem that should convince us that something is wrong is the implication of this supposedly sensible view for educational practice. In a classroom there is a concrete space, as in the library there is a kind of logical space that contains items of information. The classroom space contains students—active, sensitive, and restless organisms. On the simple location model, the function of teachers is to give the students ideas which they are to keep in mind. The ideas are thought of as workbench parts and gears; the minds on the analogy of separate cabinets in which the gears and parts are stored after they have been sorted.

The aim is, for the teacher, covering the material; for the student, speed and accuracy in information retrieval. The rigid application of this paradigm is well illustrated by the teaching of classical languages in the nineteenth century. There was initial rote memorization of the words that, in their various inflections, were the elements of the language—usually more of them than any ancient speaker ever used, or even knew. Then followed analysis of the syntax of single sentences. Finally paragraphs and verses were read and classified in terms of style and meter. In this logically impeccable form, the scheme killed off interest in the classical languages so effectively that it had to be modified. In fact, the description of Greek and Latin as dead languages was sometimes felt as more than metaphor. But the modifications were thought of concessively, as sugar-coating to enrich what was essential.

Though we think we know better now, I suspect that every teacher has worried about not covering the material, has speeded up coverage, and has come away wondering what went wrong. But it has seldom occurred to anyone that what went wrong was the presupposed notion that education meant covering the material.

Another damaging consequence of this technology of education is its deduced practical rule that maximum learning efficiency should involve minimum student-with-student interaction. For if, realistically considered, each mind to be stocked with information is as separate from every other as a Kansas silo waiting to be stocked with grain is from another in a rail-side row, contact and conversation between students can only be regarded as inefficient—as noise in both the ordinary and the technical sense. One inspired noise-reducing device is to nail each desk to the floor, and confine each student to an insulated proper place in the classroom. This is considered part of discipline.

The whole model and technology rest on a mistaken view of where things are, which has led by strict deduction to an equally mistaken view of what is really going on. But this sort of deduction about entites in space, based on this presupposition about its character, still is widespread, still fancying itself sensible.

IV

At this point, it may be helpful to go back to ancient Greece. There we find, in the classical atomic theory, the first appearance of the idea that space is a neutral insulator; and at about the same time, the antithetic view that it is a perfect superconductor. This historic topic, at any rate, is not overstudied; in 1963, Max Jammer noted that his history of concept of space was the first he knew of, and the field has seen few others since then. One virtue of going back to classical concepts is that they are often classical in their logical consistency and their purity.

Classical atomism was generated by an intersection of formal logic, ordinary sense experience, and technology. In defense of his thesis that only Being is, Parmenides argued that if there were plurality or change, there would have to be a non-Being to divide the single whole of Being into simultaneous or successive separate parts; but since he held that the statement "non-Being is" was unintelligible and without any referent, that, he thought, ended the matter. But this doctrine had the very counter-intuitive consequence that plurality and change, which seem to pervade our world, not only are unreal, but are nothing at all, hence do not even seem to be! In partial defense of this view, Parmenides' student, Zeno, showed that both science and common sense ran into paradoxes when they assumed (as they did at that time) that space and time are made up of elementary units, but still are continua. His particular line of attack was to show that taken together these views made it impossible to define and describe motion with finite velocity.

The atomists began their reasoning here. Since change does appear, they reasoned, non-Being must exist as well as pure Being. And that pure Being must come in a plurality of packets that are indivisible. These indivisible atoms escape Zeno; the non-Being postulated to accommodate Parmenides' argument that change implies not-Being becomes the space in which the particles of Being move. This space, to satisfy Parmenides' demands, must be a perfectly neutral nothing: if it had positive properties, it would be a kind of something or Being, and the old difficulty of explaining plurality would arise again.

The world view of atoms of pure Being is a spatial sea of nothing still needed to offer some explanation of causality and change. Here mechanics supplied the final notion needed to complete the theory. Clearly, the only change a classical atomist can admit of is mechanical change—his particles can transfer momentum, rebound, cling together, but that is all. And in principle, the theory held, all events can be given this type of mechanistic causal explanation.

The seventeenth century revived this notion of an insulating space, via Gassendi and Descartes, and the revived notion became generalized and built into succeeding Western common sense. (Newton's ideas were not so easily generalized and simplified.) But as Whitehead suggested, if this view of location is taken as a complete and concrete account, it works badly: for then it substitutes a highly abstract selective construct for full concrete reality. As we saw when we considered the application of this view to education, it runs into practical failures which show that something must be wrong. The theory runs into theoretical failures as well. These difficulties facing classical atomic theory are well known: secondary qualities remain inexplicable; no meaning can be given to the notion of an external world outside of the sense organs of the observer; organic time must be reversible—which it is not; we can never choose among hypotheses, since all our mental states follow from necessity, so we do not have theories, but can only report autobiographies; and so on.

With the atomic theory, Greek philosophy proposed a world of atoms and void as a way to respect logic, yet save appearance. An alternative way to escape Zeno was, of course, to have space and time be continuous, with no atomic particles whatever. Such a continuous space would be a sort of impure Being: a theater of overlapping, mixing qualities with no postulated substances underlying them (because such underlying substances would be like the impassive pure Being of Parmenides). This line of thought was pursued by Anaxagoras at about the time Democritus was working out his atomism. As the theory develops, it becomes clear that Anaxagorean space is a perfect conductor.

However, it is very important to recognize that the rejection of a Democritean view of space does not constitute a proof that space must be Anaxagorean. If there were no intermediate options, it would do that, but there are. A comparable case in modern thought would be the idea that Whitehead's rejection of simple location establishes the metaphysics of Hegel.

In some ways, Anaxagoras anticipates process philosophy. His spatial field (setting aside mind as a special case) is a continuum of overlapping qualities. There are no lines of non-Being to cut this up, since an empty space is a contradiction in terms of this view; and thus the field is a pure conductor. Like its dialectical opposite, this view breaks down pragmatically and theoretically as well. Pragmatically, the idea that size and distance make no difference in the efficiency of central control fails to work. A single Central Accounting Office for the Postal Service, the Army Quartermaster Corps, or the Soviet Russian economy, however economical it seems in Anaxagorean theory, is cumbersome and self-destructive in actual operation. On the theoretical side, we find that in a world of this kind, there is no more chance of discovering objective theories than there was in the world of atomism. The trouble this time is not that the theorist is walled off from his or her subject matter, but rather that he or she is melted into a fusion with it. When any two things are brought closer together in this space (whatever "close together" can mean) they blend and a single new third thing emerges; there is thus no standpoint that can qualify as objective. (Anaxagoras kept *nous* unmixed to avoid this objection: perhaps indeed, a divine Mind, in his scheme, would have a Pythagorean, non-perspectival view of space and time.) There is also an aesthetic, intuitive objection: that I see the desk as next to me, but I do not—as on this theory I should—identify the desk with myself. Most important, there is a moral problem, exactly the converse of the atomic theory's savage individualism: since parts lose their separate identities when they enter larger wholes—the State, the Church, the CIA—we cannot defend an ethical conviction that individuals have freedom or that persons each have responsiblity.

V

Well, then, if both of these antithetic classical views have failed, where, indeed, are things? Neither in isolated boxes, nor in one great porridge melted together. Things extend out from centers of identity, overlapping and influencing each other variably, depending on (1) the intensity of each property a thing has, (2) the relevant distance between centers in a field, and (3) the resistance or conductivity of the field in question. Each entity in space has a center of identity which holds together ("prehends" in Whitehead's vocabulary) its aspects or perspectives that spread out into the places of other persons and other things. This accounts for my feeling when I encounter a desk that the desk is really where I am, but that it has a center of identity different from mine.

It is not easy to construct an adequate diagram of this sort of modal location, and even Whitehead, expert mathematician that he was, seems never to have found a general one. Perhaps he thought that his early graphs for physics supplied the structural design for elementary cases, and that his new humanistic vocabulary in *Process and Reality* indicated a transferability from the simpler cases to more complex ones. If that is so, it seems to me he was mistaken. Of the two projects, the transfer from complex to simple entities is more plausible and clear.

While location that is neither simple nor diffuse may be hard to imagine in any detail when we populate it with atomic particles or aggregates of molecules, it becomes transparently clear when we substitute guests at a dinner for the abstract entities in a general location formula. "... Joe and George had better be separated by as many places as possible; they get noisy when they are close together ... Joe and Jane go well next to each other, but not Jane and Anne; they just gossip together." Authors and hostesses have always been sensitive to the complex overlaps and interactions of characters who meet in convivial or literary situations. But they have usually not cared about the validity of metaphysical generalizations based on their expertise. (An exception is Empedocles, whose six cosmic elements included, in addition to Earth, Air, Fire, and Water, Love and Hate.) I propose to regard these social interactions as typical cases of the way entities in space relate to each other, except that these entities have more than average sensitivity.

While I am sure that Empedocles was right in thinking that attraction and repulsion are experienced directly, I am not clear whether there is an additional literal telepathic overlapping of thoughts and feelings between selves. But even if there is not, it is clear that the extreme location concepts fail to match either sound theories, or sound practices, or sensitive intuitions.

VI

Up to this point, I have been focusing on the relation of conjunction: item by item adjunctions of entities. The ideas involved are very similar for the relations between containers and contents. When we wonder how sharply a boundary separates space into inside and outside regions, simple location again offers a tempting model. By uncritically accepting the model it offers, we mistake such relations as those of organisms to their environment, of a human self to other selves, of one sovereign state to other nations.

I want to glance at this pair of ideas—inside and outside—from the standpoint of pure mathematical topology where they are not simple even though the spaces and entities involved are purely mathematical. Then a look at pragmatic operations with inside and outside locations will be followed by a conclusion about the container-content relation in general.

A look at pure mathematics shows how far from obvious the theorem that every actuality has an inside and an outside is. For, once we have defined inside and outside by specifying that every closed curve in a plane or curved surface in a space divides the plane or space into two regions in such a way that pairs of points in different regions cannot be joined without crossing the boundary, very odd things happen. A long tube, for example, turns out to be one-sided, since by going around the

FIGURE 2.1

From Courant and Robbins, *What Is Mathematics?*, Oxford, 1941, Figure 128, p. 245. Reprinted by permission of Ernest D. Courant.

open ends, the points on the interior and the exterior can be connected without passing through the wall. The familiar one-sided Möbius strip is an even more exotic example. Common sense suggests that we can generalize our description by saying: "pairs of points differing in inside-outside location can be joined by a straight line that cuts the boundary once": but that is not true at all. For complex, zig-zag polygons (one is illustrated in Courant and Robbins, *What Is Mathematics?*, Oxford University Press, Oxford, 1941, Fig. 128, page 245), the general condition is rather that such a connecting straight line cuts the boundary an odd number of times. Thus already, in the pure non-conducting and non-insulating space of mathematics, the concepts of inside and outside prove far from simple.

That these relations might nevertheless be simple for the social spaces we inhabit is shown to be false by the evolution of the British Castle. Here, from the Norman Conquest on, a need for insulation was reflected in spatial designs intended to keep persons and property safely inside a fortification. In the 11th century, the castle design projected a simple notion of inside and outside. The inside of the castle was insulated from the rest of the world by a single high wall with square towers at the corners. Unfortunately, this is a design where a single break at any point completely destroys the inside-outside distinction. (And the higher the towers, the more easily the break can be made by mines and fire.) The prize of the British Castles—one that Cromwell could never take—was not Chepstow, high above the Severn, with its single wall; but rather a flat, polygonal fortress, Beaumarais, last built of the castles in Wales, which to the common-sense tourist looks like the most vulnerable of the lot. The castle builders progressively mastered the rules of pragmatic space. Thus, in a relatively peaceful time in the district of Kent, they devised plans in which each part of the castle is inside every other; while in the hostile world of Beaumarais, they contrived plans in which every part of the castle is outside every other part. (To do this, Beaumarais takes advantage of such devices as D-shaped half-towers, open on the inner side; so far as arrows and missiles are concerned, an enemy who has captured an outermost D-shaped half-tower, but not the inner ones, is just as effectively outside the central castle as before. The same relation holds between different levels of archers' platforms and battlements,

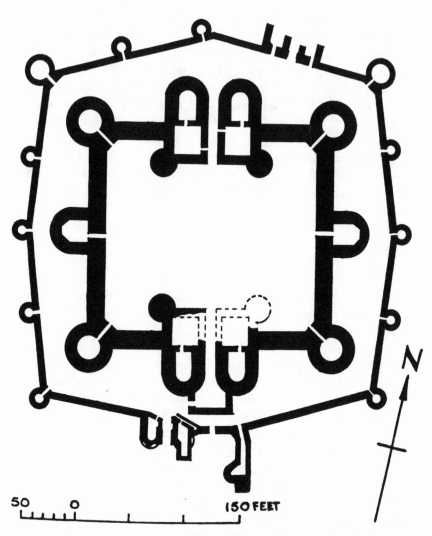

50   0   150 FEET

FIGURE 2.2

Beaumarais Castle, Anglesey, 1295-c. 1330. From B. H. St.J. O'Neil, *Castles*, Her Majesty's Stationery Office, London, 1953, p. 49. British Crown copyright; reproduced with permission of the Controller of Her Brittanic Majesty's Stationery Office.

the inner higher and overlooking the outer. The sociable design, by contrast, arranges its space about a central circular stairwell so that the rooms are all connected, while openings in the boundary—windows,

FIGURE 2.3
Walmer Castle, Kent, c. 1540. From B.H. St.J. O'Neil, *Castles*, Her Majesty's Stationery Office, London, 1953, p. 56. British Crown copyright; reproduced with permission of the Controller of Her Brittanic Majesty's Stationery Office.

gateways, gardens—break down the barrier between outer world and inner castle.)

Although pure mathematics and impure practice thus combine to suggest that living things, human selves and societies, should not be pictured on the model of Chepstow Castle—as though they were ping-pong balls, single shells that either insulate or shatter—our generalized common-sense notions of inside and outside by and large remain early Norman in their simplicity. (Two exceptions are our recognition that separately located cells are the best design for espionage and revolutionary organizations, and that round-table patterns work best for educational and convivial ones.)

An individual self is, like a social group, neither wholly private nor wholly public, but with a location vague about the edges. Clearly, a good deal of our development as selves takes place socially: through learning a language, imitating roles, identifying our feelings with those of other persons, and so on. (This is important to remember in connection with the political metaphor of national self-determination: a self there too must to some extent be created and grow; it is not innate and ready-made.) The boundaries certainly are not sharp: looking from the inside, I am pretty constant in seeing my body as part of myself; but I am not so sure about my property. Is it a substantial part of my identity? And what about my family; my country?

If I suppose a self, in this case mine, to be a simple defensive castle with my experience inside it, insulated abruptly from a not mine and not me domain outside, then what will count as important for me will be my own inner interests, pains, and pleasures. A social order, while it may be useful to protect me from invasions of privacy by other persons or from other damage by the environment, will always be external, operating by coercion. It will seem realistic to judge that my actions, as well as everyone else's, are and must be guided by calculations of self-interest, looking toward some maximum excess of pleasure over pain. And while it would give a warm emotional feeling to believe that the individual pursuit of private pleasure and the general welfare will coincide, if the insulating location model we are using is right, we can prove that this coincidence is infinitely unlikely. Suppose that the consequences of an action that will give me pleasure are nevertheless undesirable in other ways. For example, suppose that if everyone chose to act in this way, the end we aim at would be destroyed; or that, if my choice were repeated often enough, the human race would disappear. On the present view, these suppositions are ethically irrelevant, except for some inner perturbing effect they just might have. For I am not proposing that everyone else do as I do, nor even that anyone else be permitted to; their experience, like a remote future in which the human race might disappear, lies outside of my own self-interest; the inner "I" is uniquely important to me.

VII

Practically every area of human knowledge and behavior faces problems created by mistaken notions of location. In the present discussion, I have concentrated primarily on the consequences that follow from the simple location version. That is because I think these consequences are more widespread and less easily recognized than the errors that follow from the diffuse location view. In any case, the problems generated by diffuse location concepts are directly derivable from the problems consequent on the adoption of the notion of simple location simply by asserting the contrary.

Setting up an archive by mentioning in passing some of the relevant confusions, we can begin by noting that in ethics we have just seen simple location leading to radical ethical egoism. In politics it leads to ideas of nationalism—of sovereignty and self-determination—that are unrealistic and brittle. In religion, it leads to problems of God's relation to the world, to history, and to time, that become insoluble. In technology, consistent application leads to the self-destructive techniques of the efficiency expert's point of view. In aesthetics, alone, the notion has been relatively ignored and harmless: creativity has managed to remain outside the range of misguided "sensible" strait-jacketing.

VIII

One function of the philosopher is to be a critic of abstractions. Our common-sense notions of location, in the absence of that criticism, may lead us into mistaken and disastrous ideas and plans involving space and time. And since the misleading notions in question not only seem so sensible and familiar, but carry a penumbra of scientific respectability, we are often either unaware of them or wholly indisposed to question them.

Another function of the philosopher is to offer speculative alternatives to traditional positions and hypotheses. If we are not satisfied with what our current practice, science, and philosophy have to say about such a topic as space, can we propose an alternative that is more general, more coherent, more effective in practice? I think that we can.

Space is symmetrical in its mathematical, abstract form; isotropic, static, one-modal. But concrete space is entangled with acting entities and with time; and in this concrete domain the symmetries of abstract fields do not exactly match the facts of location. (It is not a mismatch, but a non-identity between the generic abstract scheme and its correct specification.) Yet the fact that there is a difference between concrete existence and philosophic abstraction does not guarantee the applicability of notions that derive their appeal from a rejection of all intellectual abstractions in favor of some anti-rational alleged intuition.

In the twentieth century, process philosophy seems to offer the most promising context for a discussion of new notions of space, place, and location—physical, social, and formal. The process orientation is not yet committed to school-wide orthodoxy regarding either the space of science or that of common sense, nor to any dogmatic identification of physical place with mathematical.

CHAPTER THREE
Sequence and Pattern

By 1925 Whitehead thought science itself had changed its basic ideas, so that it was a good time to reform a common sense that could no longer claim to be in tune with physics. Relativity theory suggested new interpretations of location and motion; quantum phenomena suggested (as of 1923 and 1924) that some sort of wave or vibration model of matter was better than the classical corpuscular view. Whitehead proposed a new philosophical treatment of space and time; glanced at some of the applications of his new views; and projected a revolutionary change in education to help bring about the needed reforms in both theoretic and practical patterns of thought.

At this same time Whitehead was also concerned to correct the popular notion that there is a necessary opposition between religion and science. It seemed to him that a new cosmology and new theology could once more bring the two into harmony. In 1929, his technical philosophical position was presented in the Gifford Lectures, a series concerned with natural theology. This is an important emphasis in *Process and Reality*: cosmology and theology are in the center of the stage, not common sense or social progress.

Whitehead's extensive influence on American speculative thought came by way of the cosmological-theological *Process and Reality*, rather than through his projects for educational reform in *The Aims of Education* and *Science and the Modern World*, or his technical work in physics, for example, in *The Principle of Relativity*. While his work with Russell in formal logic was brilliant and revolutionary, it was not proven directly relevant to problems of a more concrete kind. The result has been that process philosophy has followed Whitehead's 1929 lead, concentrating on cosmology, metaphysics, and particularly on theology, rather than developing his programs for a new philosophy of physics, social science, and education, and for the redesign of commonsense but mistaken notions of space and time. (For example, in 1978 I could name only six American theorists working with Whitehead's ideas in the field of educational theory. In physics, I can think of only two scientists who have tried to work with Whitehead's ideas in any detail, Synge and Palter. In the philosophy of science, there has been somewhat more attention [Capek, Northrop, Palter] but not very much.)

When I was invited to collaborate in a joint physics-philosophy course in space and time by my colleague Professor Frank Firk of the Yale Physics Department in the summer of 1978, it occurred to me that my contribution might be to recover and advance Whitehead's project of 1925. What I proposed to do was first generalize the ideas of space and succession from modern physics in a way that would make these concepts apply to spaces and sequences of all kinds and on all scales, social, psychological, and aesthetic as well as physics proper. This step I would describe as a transformation from the physics of space and time to the philosophy of the two.

Some precision is lost in any such generalization. To show what is gained in scope, I suggested that we think of Whitehead's proposal as replacing the fundamental observers of special relativity theory (which we had just studied) by a new class of Whiteheadian observers. Where the fundamental observers were only able to notice and report clock times of the transits of material objects across unextended spatial lines, these W-observers could also recognize qualities in various positions, and could observe patterns in time. To observe such temporal patterns, they had to be able to spatialize temporal slices of different thickness, rather than simply looking along unextended "instantaneous" lines. For example, to recognize a musical pattern of three notes, repeated, a W-observer must be able to see all three simultaneously, so that he or she will describe the repeating three-note sequence with three-note units of time—the width of the time-slice that holds the spatializable pattern. (This need to spatialize observation to get pattern recognition is a particularly interesting concept if one complements it with Bergson's rejection of modern physics, based on his insistence that spatialization always distorts and falsifies observation.) There are a number of possible differences among observers; some, for instance, are particularly expert in noticing and reporting patterns and sequences of quality. Whitehead, in fact, introduces Wordsworth and Shelley as cases in point.

From this beginning one can develop ideas of modal location, concreteness, spatial pattern, types of pattern sequence (dissipation, repetition, and reiteration), and phases of temporal existence. These new ideas can have interesting applications in an almost unlimited number of fields, although education and philosophy of history are the only two we are concentrating on. A further topic would be a recognition of the different modalities that characterize tenses or aspects of a concrete passing time. But this introduces a notion of tense that goes beyond the phases under analysis here and leads beyond the project of common sense reform into more complex issues of philosophy. (One might cite the need for logic with tenses.)[1]

In about 1925, Whitehead realized that the 17th-century scientific world view, generally accepted since, was no longer adequate for physics. This suggested to him that the view was not adequate as metaphysics either.[2] Nor was an omnipresent commonsense generalization of the 17th-centry model the only option open to social science. The early, revolutionary concepts of relativity and quantum theory forced a reconsideration of Newtonian physics and left the way open for a new philosophy.[3] The revolution in physics exposed and corrected certain evident shortcomings or paradoxes of the earlier model. These included, as Whitehead saw the catalogue, the idea of space as a perfect insulator (simple location), mechanistic determinism, secondary qualities as private fantasies going on inside a subject, temporal reversibility, matter as a kind of glass-like extended substance, and so on.[4]

Now, it is the function of philosophy to generalize special kinds of experience without falsifying them. But there are several kinds of generalization. What we want are genuine extensions of range: patterns, laws, resemblances, distinctions that help to map out a complete picture of reality. What we do not want are what Whitehead called "fallacies of misplaced concreteness": the selection of a set of abstractions from one part of experience and the arbitrary insistence that these are the only characteristics of reality in any context or domain.

Since what we want is to generalize in a proper way from modern science to re-create a relatively new philosophy, we can get to Whitehead's position by two changes in the world-view of modern physics. First, as noted earlier, we replace the fundamental observers of relativity theory with concrete perceivers (more or less like ourselves). These new observers view various time spans as their units, and are sensitive to quality as well as motion and extension. We redefine the status of observed quality to do away with the older doctrine of the subjectivity of secondary qualities. Further, the space of our new observers conducts as well as insulates, so that there is an overlap between the observer and his observed world, and between one observer and another.[5]

This generalization will give us the "philosophy of organism" based on *actual occasions* (our observers), *enduring objects* (relatively constant patterns in nature that are observed), and *processes* (to be defined presently). It can, Whitehead hoped, reconcile aspects of the world that recent Western history has arbitrarily and unhappily split apart: natural science, social existence, technological efficiency, and aesthetic value. (C. P. Snow's treatments of his "two cultures" are a sensitive documentation of the split.)[6]

The first move is a new idea of action in space, and of the W-observers that are the concrete measures in our system. We reject simple location, recognizing that reality consists of actual occasions each of which is a prehensive center of unification. An occasion holds together a set of characteristics in its neighborhood. There is no sharp line between an object and its aspects: in other words, there is no longer an absolute objective-subjective barrier. The scheme is hard to handle in detail, but in the background there may be or should be something like Russell's notion that an object is a class of perspectives. The components of an actual occasion include definite, recognizable characteristics (qualities, quantities, and so on), but also open possibilities.

A concrete entity cannot be synthesized simply by the conjunction of abstractions. Abstraction can, of course, recognize and select definite characteristics which are ingredient in the actual occasion—it just cannot exhaust them. Whitehead's picture of this relation of abstract and concrete is an inverted triangle.

We begin with the notion of an actual occasion, *alpha*, holding together a set of properties (eternal objects) around its center in space and time.

By repeated abstraction, we can find a set of simple eternal objects. The set of these, g, is the base of the abstractive hierarchy derived from *alpha*. (Thus we get the set, g, of eternal objects of grade zero: A B C D E F. . . .)

However, these properties do not occur in *alpha* automically and separately, but in combination. For example, if A is red and B is triangularity, the compound property *alpha* exhibits will be A & B. We can think of these compounds as vertexes of hierarchies based on the set g. Thus, we get hierarchies of level 1 combining level 0 eternal objects.

A   B   C   D
                  —abrupt hierarchies of level 1
   A&B   C&D

The process can go on to a complexity of level 2:

A&B   C&D . . . .
             —abrupt hierarchy of level 2
    (A&B) & (C&D)

This can continue indefinitely, to level n:

A   B   C   D
  A&B   B&C   C&D
    (A&B)&(C&D)   (B&C)&(C&D)
        *level n

But each of these is abrupt; it has a definite, denumerable set of components. And between the abrupt hierarchy of level n, and the concrete occasion, *alpha*, there is a gap.

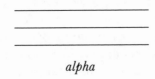

alpha

41

The full content of *alpha*, which is not exhausted by adding finite properties from the abrupt hierarchies associated with it, is called the "associated hierarchy of *alpha*." This cannot be defined, nor constructed; but it can be appreciated intuitively.

Along the top are the eternal objects of grade 0 that are present in the actual occasion. These are repeatable, definable, and simple; they look rather like the simple ideas of British empiricism. At the bottom vertex lies the concrete occasion, *alpha*. The entire set of definite characteristics which alpha holds grouped about it is the associated hierarchy of alpha; and it is infinitely complex. The eternal objects that come into *alpha* form various abstract combinations: for example, if A is red, and B a triangle, a red triangle is the complex eternal object, A.B (where "." indicates "and"). These various sets are also hierarchies, which converge to a most complex member; Whitehead calls them "abrupt hierarchies." They represent various selective abstractions of the characteristics of *alpha*. One point important for the development of the theory using a generalization of the notion of observer is that our conscious awareness of characteristics is always selective and finite.[7] An observer with a mind is mentally aware of a finite set of related abstract properties, not of the fully concrete occasion. We also, however, have intuition and feeling through which we recognize the difference between the abstract (however complex) and the fully concrete (however locally limited).

We may note here that there are three main kinds of abrupt hierarchies that can be abstracted from occasions. These are the hierarchies of taxonomic abstraction (properties organized into schemes of classification), pragmatic abstraction (properties sorted out in terms of useful operation), and conscious attention (properties that we notice in perception).[8] A logician will note that there are three kinds of limitation built into this scheme. On the level of eternal objects, there are rules of possible combinations in a purely logical domain; on the level of space-time relations, there are additional requirements, since fewer patterns can be together in space and time than can in a realm of pure possibility; and in the shape of a given individual occasion, there are still other limitations operating—an inherited past, for example, and a context of forces from other occasions.[9]

Before we summarize what we have said so far, four points should be

---

emphasized. First, a concrete entity cannot be duplicated by adding up abstractions; and we will find that value always attaches to the concrete. Second, an actual entity can equally well be defined as its aspects in other objects or as its patterned characters about a prehensive center. Third, actual occasions act on one another; their actions correspond to, among other things, gravitational or electromagnetic forces in their common field. Fourth, among the ingredient objects in an occasion we must include some future possibilities, though it is not yet clear how.

At this point, we can read Whitehead's own account of science and poetry from the 17th century to the 20th as a study of the observers that have been involved or presupposed. The scheme runs from the mind/body dualism of Descartes through the wholly passive observer of Hume to the unexpectedly active observer of Kant who builds a good deal of structure into his world in the course of observing it. Various idealisms, which Whitehead jumps over, try to generate the natural world from some postulated mind; but the natural world they generate is still exactly that of 17th-century science, where mind is not at home. The poets of the 19th century are introduced as special observers, and their immediate intuitions are used to test the general organic scheme of actual occasions and eternal objects.[10]

Wordsworth and Shelley prove elegant choices for Whitehead's purposes. Not only do they offer evidence for his central point that value is actually ingredient in nature, but they offer two special insights that match the metaphysics Whitehead built on the foundations of new natural science. Whitehead's starting point is the concrete occasion, holding together a pattern of characteristics, called "eternal objects." If the center loses its ability to hold the parts together, the pattern will fly apart as the released properties either fly to another prehensive center, or retreat to some reservoir of possibility. Shelley's repeated imagery of change and fragmentation reports his sensitivity to this dissipation of pattern; Wordsworth's pantheistic notion of the mutual grasping of the concrete actualities of nature reports his sensitivity to the enduring objects in nature and their connections with one another.[11]

Turning now to time, we find that existence itself is a process of modification of pattern. There are three general kinds of pattern change. When a given pattern loses its stability, and cannot regroup, it dissipates—dissipating patterns are transitory and unstable. Atomic fission is probably the most spectacular case that comes to mind here. Or, if the pattern is relatively stable, it may repeat after it has been dislocated. Repeating patterns produce enduring objects; these have relative stability, but only the single pattern, hence no adaptability. On the one hand, their stability represents a limited achievement of value; but it also excludes other patterns which might be more valuable. The third possibility for progression of pattern is reiteration. This is not literal repetition, but modified, in the way a variation reiterates a musical theme. Where pattern is reconstituted, but modified, we have process—a clear example is the pattern of animal evolution as observed in zoology.

Each episode of pattern disturbance and modification consists of three "phases of concrescence" in Whitehead's technical philosophy. First, there is some encounter, some change in equilibrium that deforms a pattern; second, there is a period of readjustment of parts; third, there is a new stabilization which marks the end of that event. At this third point, the recaptured pattern is closed and past; it has objective immortality; it is inherited by its successor events, but it itself is fixed and unchanging.

It is interesting to note that comparison of spatial patterns offers a key to understanding some types of temporal sequence. The reason is that a pattern change representing a continuing movement toward or away from a prehensive center will continue unless new external forces are applied. Thus the tendency toward decentralization of the college and the professional schools for the University of Connecticut at Storrs can be seen in maps a decade apart, which show the Law School established in Hartford, the Medical School in Farmington, etc. In the same way, sequential maps of cities show patterns of steady concentric expansion of population, until other factors change the forces at work. Or, as is the case with modern Athens, a central attraction may be so strong that the peripheral objects—in this case, persons—cannot keep their distance, and are crushed into the center. For Athens, this is a population movement which has emptied the more remote countryside.

Thus there are laws of pattern sequence which fall between the spatial study of fixed pattern and the process study of emerging pattern. We might call this intermediate realm the study of sequential pattern, where a rule can be given relating each spatial section to its predecessors by a functional connection. Such patterns will stay the same in structure, but change constantly in scale, until they reach "catastrophic" limiting values, to use a mathematical expression. The changes may be the result of negative as well as positive prehension. Thus some patterns fly apart when there is repulsion between the center and its peripheral aspects. As noted above, Empedocles had already, with poetic insight, recognized this when among his elements he included not only earth, air, fire, and water, but also love and hate. Even more interesting, and perhaps, more in keeping with the changing dynamics suggested by process philosophy, are sequences of patterns where successive pairs are related by constantly changing dynamics, for example, their rates of acceleration (third derivatives with respect to clock time).

In fact, however, in Whitehead's world, repetition and constant pattern expansion or contraction in sequence are only approximated. Over a sufficient span of sequence, what seemed literal repetition or predictable change of scale turns out to have been reiteration, an organic process rather than a merely mechanical recurrence.

And, although it is an extension that Whitehead never explicitly made, one could argue that every process, viewed with an appropriate width of space-and-sequence scale, shows the phases of concrescense that characterize Whiteheadian one-way time. In connection with these time patterns, note that: dissipating patterns are neither reversible nor repeatable; patterns of endurance are both reversible and repeatable; patterns of process are one-directional and not repeatable.[12]

Whitehead can now extend the general analysis of pattern to larger and more complex entities and processes. For example, on the scale of an individual person, a human learning experience has this same phase pattern. It begins in a stage of romance, proceeds through a stage of precision, and ends with the satisfaction of mastery, of a successfully grasped generalization. The student who has just encountered a translated passage from *Beowulf* may decide that this is an epic he or she must read. To follow up this decision, it is necessary to learn the part-by-part items that make up skill in Anglo-Saxon. Finally, the two phases come together when the student can read the epic with technical facility and literary appreciation.[13]

A society, too, on its scale has these phases of pattern sequence. Whitehead, in passing, indicates this by his remark that five ideas define civilization: truth, beauty, adventure, art, and peace. The first two terms represent necessary conditions: an actual environment and an awareness of a possible ideal. The next three are the phases of concrescence again. Some impact jolts the established pattern, and a society must dissipate, or regroup, or advance. The phase of art seems to be a progressive adjustment and interaction of the parts that make up a civilization when they reinforce, rather than neutralize, one another. Finally, the stage of peace, like the satisfaction that ends an event on the small-scale level, marks a restabilization, the end of an era. If there is no new disturbance, a pattern from this stage of peace may endure, but as it endures it loses its creativity and adaptability, and the civilization declines. A social pattern that merely repeats is not going to offer achievements that count as civilization; clearly, neither will an order that dissipates.[14]

This general idea of pattern transmission can apply to phenomena as different in scale as the vibrations of an atomic clock and the elevation and erosion of a mountain range, or the evolution of galaxies and stars. We ourselves seem about at the center. (The atomic clock's period is 10^{-9} seconds; our own brain waves run at about 10^{-1} seconds; our life span is on the order of 10^7 seconds; the mountain range phases are about 10^{12} seconds; a civilization runs its course in 10^8 seconds; and so on.)

From pattern our course passed to time. We began with Whitrow's distinction between Archimedean and Aristotelian time. We needed to explore the Aristotelian variety, a t that not only has phases and directions and patterns, but aspects and modalities as well.[15]

Appendix

We can learn something about the presuppositions of science and the history of philosophy by seeing what different Western philo-

46

sophies conceive the perfect observer, God, to be like.

For one class of theories, God's omniscience consists in his seeing reality spatialized, structured by mathematical invariants. For this view, there is no basic difference between space and time; it is due to imperfection that the human observer finds the two different.[16] For a second class, an omniscient being knows all the natural kinds of things and all the natural cycles that there are: a vision of unchanging types and cyclic patterns. (This is nearly spatial again: for a cycle admits no distinction of before and after, and for the thing moving in it, the only distinction is between a moment that is "now" and the rest that are "not now." God, however, sees the cycles as unmoving and at rest; hence He does not know this "now" vs. "not now" distinction.[17]) A mechanistic world of particles in interaction has suggested all kinds of major and minor deities: Laplace's demon, Clarke's clockmaker, and the rest. These gods are all able to calculate causal sequences through a linear time which is in principle reversible, and in which future facts are predetermined.[18] These observers pick up quantitative properties, but not qualitative. Finally, a Whiteheadian God sees a world in process, a world where new modifications of concrete pattern emerge through reiteration, a world where temporal passage is irreversible.[19]

CHAPTER FOUR
Logic and Time

Since Plato set up his description of the ideal curriculum in his *Republic*, we have thought of formal logic and pure mathematics as ways of teaching students "how to think." There is no doubt that these studies are useful in that connection, though whether Plato's recommendation that ten years study of pure mathematics be required training for all future legislators may be more questionable.

However, there is a radical difference between the world we live in and the world that logic and mathematics talk about. Patterns and numbers are an abstract domain, linked by necessary connections, beyond space and time. As a result, logical implications need not be dated; truth values can be treated as invariant; premises are accepted as hypotheses. But how often do human affairs lend themselves to demonstrations beyond possible contingency or doubt? Logical proof is applicable to timeless contexts, and sometimes it can single out temporal impossibilities; but the notion that causal patterns through time have the austere necessity of causality in the way logical patterns do is sheer illusion. The illusion is the result of the illicit extension of the seventeenth-century notion of causality in physics to causality generally, assuming that it is always and everywhere predictable, predetermined, and necessary.

G. J. Whitrow, in his *Natural Philosophy of Time*, opens by contrasting two time concepts which he calls Archimedean and Aristotelian. Archimedean time is a mathematician's delight; a tidy fourth dimension, reversible, homogeneous. Aristotelian time is messy, a field of growth and change, one-directional and perversely divided into a past that has necessity and a future marked by contingency. We live in Aristotelian time, and it does our students doubtful service to equip them without warning with tools that assume all time to be Archimedean.

One of my former students in Maine, an enthusiastic symbolic logician (in an era when this symbolism was still rather new) became a high-school principal. He at once set about teaching his students a new course in how to think. In particular, his theme was that patterns of proof which are less than necessarily so should be avoided. In the next classroom, and in fact in the next period, a civics class was studying American law. It turned out that not one of the principles of our political system, their application, or the decisions of courts based on available evidence, met the standards of indubitable proof. When last I heard about my student, the report was that he had changed his course to one on ethics.

(We don't make too much of the point, but ordinary verification procedures fail to satisfy the criteria of strict logic. If p implies q, we predict q, and look for it. This is the pattern of crucial experiments in science, and critical evidence in law. But p does not necessarily follow from "p implies q, and q". All such reasoning is, strictly, not logical.)

Excellent as logic and mathematics are for training in abstract thought, their use contains a dangerous invitation to identify the abstract with the concrete. In particular, there is no room for choices in time, or for contingencies. The incorrect assumption is made that every proposition is either true or false, regardless of the date and time reference of its assertion. Aristotle (working in Aristotelian time) had already noted, some time ago, that this assumption presupposes absolute determinism in nature, and denies any human freedom.

A formal modification of logic, taking account of a set of distinctions that Whitehead made in his cosmology, but never went back to add to the system of *Principia Mathematica*, can correct this confusion. It is a correction crucial for what follows later in my discussion regarding the direction of time, the need for concrete seeing, and the true importance of each human individual.

The reader who dislikes formal tables, however, may want to take the claim on faith that formal systems can be easily modified to take account of Aristotelian as well as Archimedean time, and move ahead to see the other educational implications of the non-Archimedean concepts.

Just to illustrate the point, let me take a simple problem. A penny has come up heads twenty times in twenty tosses. What is the probability that it will be tails on a twenty-first throw? A mathematician or statistician answers at once that this is $1/2$, and assumes that the coin is unbiased. A naive gambler, realizing that the chance of 21 heads in a row is $1/2^{21}$ will bet his entire fortune on tails, overlooking the fact that he is not betting on sets of 21 tosses, where those odds apply, but to a single toss. He, too, assumes a fair coin, but mis-reasons: pure logic can help him. A normal human being doubts the assumption that any coin which comes up heads twenty times straight is a fair coin, and bets heavily on heads again for the twenty-first throw. There is a way, in pure probability theory, to educate our second character, so that he will not continue to commit the typical gambler's fallacy. But there is no way to show the man of common sense that his behavior is either logical or illogical: runs of twenty heads with fair coins are of course possible, and nothing in the formal system requires us to change the assumption that the coin is fair, but its behavior temporarily unlikely!

Ordinarily, a logic with tenses seems unnecessary. Science, theology, and politics have evolved methods of prediction and decision based on patterns which, in outline, mathematical logic has generalized. However, there are different implicit kinds of time-reference involved in different fields of application; these cause no trouble except when a problem crosses boundaries, transferring one time-reference rule to another area where it does not apply. Another way of stating this is that it is only when metaphysical questions are asked that logic with tenses is needed. But these problems are not arcane or unimportant; on the contrary.

As a beginning, consider the perennial ethical and legal problem of freedom versus determinism in the context of the relation of expert testimony to criminal law. As psychiatry and social science develop greater explanatory power, we seem destined to defend any criminal action on the basis of irresistible impulse. A legal psychology which talks about a corrupt will will run the risk of being dismissed as unscientific and anachronistic and jurisprudence will be replaced by sociology. Kant had the correct diagnosis of this effect. Since knowledge is possible only by presupposing unbroken and determined lines of cause and effect, a genuine incoherence of the phenomenal order cannot be imagined or observed. A free agent could never recognize himself or herself in this mirror of the phenomenal order. As a result, ethics and law, which rest on imperatives, derive from a different level of reality from science, and employ a different method.[2]

However, the more satisfying explanation of freedom and determinism coexisting is rather that scientific statements are verifiable and meaningful only with reference to past, and ethical statements to present, tenses. ("Aspect" might be a better word than "tense" here since it is evident that scientists make predictions and ethicists discuss past decisions.) Their respective discussions presuppose different degrees of determinateness. The scientist, talking about an eclipse of the moon in the future, is speaking from a standpoint still further future, thinking about observations and data that will constitute the eclipse once it has become past. This is Bergson's central point, of course, in his *Time and Free Will*.[3] The ethicist, discussing Socrates on trial, stands in the court with Socrates in the aspect of a present moment when alternative options for moral decision remain. It is not an accident, but built into the logic of the situation, that the one finds only necessity in the future while the other finds freedom in the past.

One of the most evident properties of time is that the past is a locus of facts, while options are future or present. A method of observation which accepts nothing short of determinate fact cannot admit the less determinate option or the even more evanescent possibility. Analogous logical patterns surely hold for any degree of determinateness; but since they are the same only by analogy, there may be unexpected trouble in running transitive inferences from one aspect to another.

I suppose there could be worlds in which there was no difference between the aspects of present and past. But in our actual world, it is impossible to deny this difference without falling into a self-referential absurdity—not purely logical. Throughout Western thought, determinists have explained and argued for determinism by taking a present aspect as their relation to the reader—thereby contradicting themselves. The Stoic view, for example, that all is determined adds, except our attitudes. The classical atomist tells us that mechanical chains of causality determine everything from all eternity, then adds: "we ought to accept this as true theory." The scientist exploring determinism in human behavior tells with some pride what controls he chose to use in his experiment.[4] Philosophers have wished that their ideas be considered as though their own existence and behavior were wholly irrelevant. It is puzzling to see how much they have gotten away with in the past; for when the philosopher's existence and thought presuppose the contradictory of his or her theory, we are entitled to judge that he or she is not telling us the whole truth. But perhaps from Democritus to Spencer the West has had too poor an opinion of philosophy to expect it to apply.[5]

Confronted, however, by apparent contradictions between psychiatry and legal psychology, anthropology and ethics, expediency and justice, the West had best revise its low estimate of philosophy and quickly solve these problems. A cross-field logic which takes account of degrees of determinateness may give a perspicuous formal pattern useful in diagnosis and inquiry. The difficulty is probably in interpretation rather than in design: below, I present an extremely simple and abstract class-calculus with tenses which almost provides the exact theorems needed to differentiate and cross the lines between past, present, and future aspects. I consider this agreement between formal simplicity and incredible phenomenal complexity of time an encouraging omen for future developments of tensed logic, and beyond this, it is a fact of more than passing metaphysical interest.

To begin with, let $= 1$ and $= 0$ stand for determinate emptiness and determinate completeness. But there is a range of other degrees of determination, from which we choose two. Let $\neq 0$ represent the range of values greater than 0, not excluding $= 1$; and let $\neq 1$ represent the values less than 1, not excluding 0. For the present, there is no harm in thinking of these as truth-values. What must be kept in mind, however, is that $\neq 0$ and $\neq 1$ refer to ranges, and hence give limited information. They indicate that a value is known to be within this range; they do not indicate that it has a determinate exact fractional value; though neither do they indicate that it does not.

The resulting system differs from others of a like kind in two ways. First, it is not modal in the usual sense of offering only three modalities; it can in principle accommodate any number of degrees of determinateness.[6] Second, the use of both $\neq 0$ and $\neq 1$ distinguishes between two sets of possibilities, the confusion of which has caused difficulties in Western philosophy. Among future events, regarded purely as future, there is an indeterminacy and overlap which does not easily admit of formal articulation. All of these, I will call "possibilities," and define as the class of referents of propositions which from their aspect have a truth-value of $\neq 1$. The law of contradiction applies in a peculiar way here, since p and $\sim$ p are compossible.[7] (Both a possible statue of Hermes and its complement are in this marble, to use Aristotle's example.) But no sooner does Leibniz, or Whitehead, or perhaps Anaxagoras introduce a realm of such possibilities than he discovers that not all of these are really possible. That is, there are two additional demands made on a real possibility. First, it must conform to the past when it emerges in space and time; second, it must be close enough to the present so that it can be chosen to the exclusion of other possibles. Selected possibilities on hand for present choice, I call "options": the propositions about them all have the value $\neq 0$. Compared to the vague expanse of compossible future entities, their existence is already somewhat determinate.

In other words, the inequations will be treated as incomplete truth specifications, locating p somewhere within a range. The reason for doing this is that it is desirable to have a system which does not begin by accepting some strong commitment about the existence of precise fractional truth-values. It may not be necessary to know whether these always exist and in some sense stay the same; or whether, in some cases, they are not as yet exactly determined. Although in what follows we will talk in terms of the second of these options, it should be remembered that an equally relevant interpretation can be given by translation into the language of the first.

This scheme requires an enlarged truth table, set up in three parts. The first four rows are the standard definite combinations of 0 and 1. The next five have $\neq 1$ as a value for p, or q, or both. This is section II. The last seven rows have $\neq 0$ as a value for p, or q, or both. This is section III. Given this reference table of combinations, we define a negation ($\sim$ p) as the value that definitely falsifies p, as in column 3. Disjunction as defined holds fractionally, as in column 4. We also set up columns for p v $\sim$p (column 5), for $\sim$p v q (column 7), and p v $\sim$p (column 6).

1 (ref.)		2	3	4	5	6	7
p	q	~p	p ⊃ q	p · [p ⊃ q] ⊃ q	p v ~p	~p v q	6 ≡ 3
1	1	0	1	1	1	1	1
1	0	0	0	1	1	0	1
0	1	1	1	1	1	1	1
0	0	1	1	1	1	1	1
1	≠1	0	≠1	≠1	1	≠1	1
0	≠1	1	1	1	1	1	1
≠1	1	1	1	1	1	1	1
≠1	0	1	d	d	1	d	1
≠1	≠1	1	*	*	1	*	1
1	≠1	≠0	≠0	≠0	1	≠0	1
0	1	1	1	1	≠1	1	1
≠0	≠0	0	≠0	≠0	≠0	1	1
≠0	0	0	0	0	≠0	0	1
≠1	≠1	1	≠1	≠1	1	≠0	1
≠0	≠1	0	≠1	≠1	≠0	≠1	1
≠0	≠0	0	≠0	≠0	≠0	≠0	1

This expansion can now be given a tense interpretation. Let ≠ 1 represent a *possibility*, a future situation that may not come about. Then section II gives the combinations of the *past* or *atemporal* values (exclusively used in section I), with distinctively *future* values. Let ≠ 0 represent a *contingency*, a present option that is not impossible. Then section III displays the truth relations between *present* and past or future propositions.

Several features of this interpretation are suggestive. With the definition of negation we are using (such that p . ~p is never = 1), the law (p v ~p) holds determinately for both past and future time. This is the property of exhaustive disjunctions with future reference that Aristotle singled out in his sea-fight tomorrow.[8] The relation does not hold determinately for all cases of contingency, however. It is never determinately or possibly false for any of these cases, except ≠ 0. This characterizes cases where a present option is genuine, and therefore has some degree of determinateness greater than 0, though that degree may not increase. In these cases, the truth-value will change back to 0 as the contingency transforms into part of a determinate past, in which (p v ~p) holds definitely. (Many philosophic systems need to differentiate pure possibility from realizable or relevant possibility. It seems better to do it in the present way than to eliminate one of these possibilities in favor of the other, or to eliminate both in favor of actuality.)

Modus ponens holds determinately for past and atemporal relations. It may be false, though it is never determinately false, when we try to use it to connect past and future. It may be only fractionally true (though never determinately false) when it bridges past-or-atemporal and present, present and future, or present and present. This is again an Aristotelian result. For in the *Organon*, Aristotle rejected inferences from antecedent to consequent by efficient causes, on the ground that these were not necessarily valid when the consequent was future.[9] Aristotle also should have rejected them when the consequent was only a present contingency; for in these cases, it seems that his rule that a possible A implies a possible E (in his sense of possible) rules out determinate demonstration. The present, and any future possibility that can become actual, must be compatible with the past, but need not be wholly determined by it.

A further interesting property of this table interpreted as a calculus with tenses is the behavior of $(p . \sim p)$. This is determinately false except where the tense of one proposition is future: there it is indeterminate $(\neq 1)$. This matches our actual experience with, for example, an artist's medium.[10] Contradictory possibilities are present there, though one or the other will become actual. And the material implication relation (in its usual sense of not proven disconnected which is what we want here), shows an unexpected definiteness of value when a false proposition about the past is connected to an indeterminate present or future proposition.[11] It is definite and $= 1$, which means that a past that did not and does not exist cannot be proven actually disconnected from present or future. Inferences from present or future to an actual past show definite values $(= 1)$, but inferences forward from definite past to present or future show indefinite ones $(\neq 1, \neq 0)$. Our material implication relation has another property, interpretable as connectedness, or lack of it, between present and future or past. For $p \supset q$, where p is a contingency $(\neq 0)$ and q is false $(= 0)$, $p \supset q = 0$; no actual connection holds. For $p \supset q$, where p is a possibility $(\neq 1)$, and q is false $(= 0)$, we get the result that $p \supset q$ has the definite but undetermined value $d(= 0 \text{ v} = 1)$. From the standpoint of the future possibility, a non-actual past thus comes out definitely but not determinately related. (This is a metaphysical curiosity; I suspect it has been noted and taken as typical of all future-past relations by logicians who hold that tenses are irrelevant, and logic can handle them using only the determinate values 0 and 1.)

It can be seen that my four-valued propositional calculus catches some of the structure of actual time. (1) It admits both the exhaustiveness and possible compresence of contrary future possibilities. (2) It recognizes the indefiniteness of relations which move from past or atemporal antecdents to present or future consequents. (3) It differentiates the types of connections that hold between present, future, and actual and non-actual past. So far, so good. But we need a great deal more before we can claim any exact fit between such a tense-system and actual time as we experience it.

Some formal relations are more puzzling, and perhaps less welcome. The law, $p \vee \sim p$, holds determinately for past and future, but not for $\neq 0$, where it is only partially definite. This may be a result of lack of adequate information; since $\neq 0$ includes the case of $= 1$, more information (e.g., the axiom that $p + \sim p$ is always $= 1$) could clear up this inconvenient result. Second, two values in the table are $*$, two are d. The d value first appears as a new value ($= 1 \vee = 0$) which holds when we try to determine the connection between a possibility and a non-existent past or false abstract proposition. In these cases, we need to know more about $\neq 1$: if it is also $\neq 0$ (enough in touch with past and present to offer some degree of definiteness as an option), it cannot imply a non-existent past. But if the possibility in itself cannot become an option at any time, it can imply anything at all, including false-hoods and non-facts. Similarly, the value $*$ indicates that not enough information is given by the statement "p is possible, and q is possible" to determine the compossibility of p and q. The upshot is that these ambiguities could be eliminated if we had suitable additional axioms characterizing the type of order that limits the domains of possibility and option.[12]

This is the reason for the objectionable stickiness of logics with an indefinite as one of three truth-values, and probably the main reason why there has been so little follow-up of Prior's splendid beginning exploration of logic with tenses.[13] We have only three choices: either

(1) we assume the realms of option and possibility to be ordered exactly as those of fact and abstraction are, in which case we revert to the simple two-valued table and lose time; or (2) we make no assumption about their types of order, in which case our logical relations gradually muddle up and lose all definiteness; or (3) we recognize that compossibility and means-end are ordered domains, but not in the same way as past and abstract; then we need to study their order. If in taking the third way there still remains some ambiguity, the fault is not with our formal system but the world that system is about.[14]

There remains the problem of formulating a law that time progresses, so that the future becomes present, and the present becomes past. The natural way to try this is: pt $0 \neq 1 \supset$ pt $0 + n = 1$ v $= 0$; pt $0 \neq 0 \supset$ pt $0 + n = 1$ v $= 0$; pt $0 + n = 1$ v $= 0$; pt $0 \neq 1$. The first part states that some time in the future, a possibility with future location now (i.e., at t 0) p $\neq 1$ will either become actual or become non-actual, i.e., impossible. The second rule is that present options take on definiteness as they become past facts. The third rule states that the past is completely definite; the fourth, that the present need not be. Oddly enough, the ambiguity we find in this abstract scheme is exactly what we found infecting ordinary language: it does not know which point on our ordered scale is now, but only says "if we are now here, then the division between definiteness and indefiniteness comes where we are."[15]

This leaves open the possibility that t0 is different for different observers, so that one can verify as completely determinate and past what for another is still problematic and future. This contradicts the notion that now is the same for every observer. But as long as there is time, in our sense of a continuous transformation of possibility into fact, we want a degree of definiteness to be a property of the situations and things we refer to, and satisfy the condition that one referent has only one degree of definiteness at any time. We might do this by adding the rule that t0 is the same for every observer. No harm results, formally, from this condition; but what effect does it have on our interpretation? We still do not know where t0 is. But even so, we are now committed, I think, to a new interpretation of omniscience, in science and theology. Neither a Laplacian calculator nor a Christian God can know something which is actually indeterminate. That is, a perfect knowledge for any t0 will include knowledge of contingencies only so far as they are actual; omniscience does not involve knowing things as they are not—for example, seeing the future as though it were past. The difficulty we have in understanding this consequence is significant. The reason is that there are all sorts of cases in which observers do differ in their beliefs as to the location of t0. This direction of inquiry leads, however, into psychology and phenomenology; I shall put it aside for a future occasion.

From what has been presented, several conclusions follow. The first is that a logic taking account of degrees of definiteness, which can then be interpreted as aspect or tense time-locations, is remarkably simple to devise—simple at least in a first approximation. The second is that this formal apparatus is needed only when problems and inferences cut across aspect lines: that is, when an explanation that tacitly assumes the definiteness of past events is applied to present situations, or vice-versa. Traditionally, these problems probably would have been called "metaphysical." But whatever their name, they do exist, and are of such practical importance that they urgently need expert study.

Let me present some of these cross-boundary problems. The first set occurs when a present that has alternative options is treated on the model of the past, where all options are closed. This takes place, for example, in criminal law cases where an expert psychologist or social scientist argues that there is no possibility of the criminal having done otherwise; but the jury and the judge remain persuaded that before his action, the criminal had a choice open and chose wrongly. More spectacular is the problem of whether the social sciences should be content with a method and world-view developed in the physical sciences. The humanist often protests that social engineering may result from this transfer of method, thereby destroying freedom, authenticity, and creativity, all of which are potentially attainable. And from our difficulty in defining t0, it is clear that there is also a theological application of tense logic. If it is inherently impossible for there to be omniscience as simultaneous knowledge of all history in full concrete detail, this may well be the key to the classical problem of pre-destination and free-will. This point is one made persuasively by Whitehead. It also follows, from the difficulties we have seen, that individual persons can differ drastically in their actual time-location.

This is an actual fact, not a mere possibility; and some of its implications are being discussed now in psychology. The ambiguity of ordinary language is eloquent testimony here to the fact that collective human experience has been unable to decide what time standpoint it is most pragmatically effective to observe; on close analysis, its openness may be less great than I expect; but the apparent neutrality certainly poses a problem.

CHAPTER FIVE
Time Passes: Platonic Variations

KAI POREUETAI HO CHRONOS? NAI. Plato, *Parmenides*.

The purpose of this chapter is a double one. I want to show, in the first place, how a Platonic attempt to describe the structure of time that we encounter in becoming presupposes a reference to the more stable structure of the realm of being. The result of this presupposition is a temptation to substitute the more stable forms for the less intellectually congenial ones, thus turning time into a dimension of space or a series of arithmetical units. This can only be corrected by reversing normal Platonic explanatory direction and explaining the appearances of time on the several levels of the Platonic cosmos by adding increments of non-being and irregularity to the pure forms of arithmetic and geometry. In the second place, this Platonic explanation shows exactly why an appeal to the structure of language is of no help whatever in determining the nature of time, real or apparent. Because the attempt is so often made to start with language structure as a key to time, I consider my demonstration that this is misguided an important one.[1] I concede that my discussion of the issue is radically Platonic. The reason is in part the elegance with which the Platonic system locates talking about time on the level of *eikasia*, the realm of shadows on the wall of Plato's Cave.[2]

Of course, if we take Platonic forms as our paradigm of reality, time is unreal; and so are the objects and persons immersed in a time that passes. Becoming has an admixture of non-being in it; while it can

Reprinted by permission of the editor of *The Review of Metaphysics*, XXXIII (1980): 711–726. Copyright by *The Review of Metaphysics*, published by the Philosophy Education Society, Inc.

imitate eternal order, it does so only by projecting it into modal sequence. My interest here is therefore not the question of the reality of time, but of the kinds of unreality which mix with being to constitute time.

The admixture of unreality in each lower level of time is shown by the fact that we can perceive it, talk about it, or measure it only by relating and contrasting each type to the next higher level in the being-to-becoming hierarchy. Thus we think that subjective time, though time-like, is eccentric—because we try to correlate it with the more regularly paced biological time in which we are inexorably growing older. But that growing older, itself, needs for its recognition a background of objective time: a public time which stays constant as we age; the cyclic time of clock and calendar. It is by contrast with this that we recognize how our aging seems to cause changes in the length of seasons and of years—a contrast that requires a frame of fixed years and seasons. But the regularity of the cycles of seasons and years is itself comprehensible only against the backdrop of a space-like dimension, a field by which to define congruence and distance. This level is in fact close to the Platonic form of time; but in the ascent to this pure reality, time has lost all temporality. We must go again to the Demiurge's mixing bowl and mix new batches of matter, second, third, and fourth in purity, as the receptacles of becoming. These mixtures embody the successive incarnations of the descent of being into passing time. It is the fourth degree of impure mixture that presents us with time in language; and since, to borrow Aristotle's way of stating the case, the order of what is obvious to us and what is obvious in reality are the opposite of one another, philosophers are misguided when it is with a concentration on language that they all too often not only commence, but conclude, analyses of time.

The Platonic starting-point of this enterprise is the postulate that becoming has peculiar logical structures of its own. We are dealing with projected, weakened vestiges of the perfect, static order of the number series and geometrical figures. Can we say how far, and in what way we need to weaken the law of identity to get a formal statement of the degree to which static order applies to things in time that passes? How many kinds of temporal increments can we find if we look for interpretations of *delta t* in abstract formulas? Why does our natural desire for clarity operate to make us talk and think about time spatially? Do the stretching, varying events and states of our private subjective worlds still preserve traces of the form of time; and, if so, can we control their sequence to create more time? These questions are particularly interesting in connection with a range of large-scale, hard to define problems in educational theory, metaphysics, abnormal psychology, and theology. And one thing that contributes to the difficulty is failure to recognize that time passes at more than one rate, in more than one way.[3]

In the previous chapter, I suggested that two conditions must be satisfied by any time that passes. These are: (1) There must be a "now" which divides a past of fixed actualities from a future of not-wholly-definite possibilities; (2) and "now" divides successively as successive increments of passage are added. As a simple way to represent these conditions, we can use a formal table of definiteness values, V, for propositions with time reference.[4] In this schema, all propositions with *past* time referents (past relevant to the present time of their assertion, t0) have the definiteness values $V = 0$ or $= 1$, while those with *future* reference (again relative to t0) have the indefinite value $\neq 1$. (I further suggest that for *present* reference the indefinite value $\neq 0$ applies.) Then a three-part rule will take account of passage:

(1) $V(p)t0 \neq 0 \supset (V(p)t0{+}dt = 0 \quad v \quad = 1)$

(2) $V(p)t0 \neq 1 \supset (V(p)t0{+}ndt = 0 \quad v \quad = 1)$

(3) $V(p)t0 = (1 \, v \, 0) \supset (V(p)t0{+}ndt = V(p)t0)$

These patterns are not quite self-explanatory, but they are not mysterious either. Without being more technical than the idea requires, we can think of "definiteness values" (V) as the degree to which statements correspond to the actual present conditions of their referents. Since the past is fixed, statements referring to past time (t–) are definite, either 1 or 0; and no number (n) of added increments of time (dt) will change this. (This is the implication of (3).) On the other hand, a proposition about the future is usually neither impossible nor certain; and we represent this by $\neq 1$. However, given enough increments of time (ndt), this proposition will—when its referent becomes past—become definite, with 1 or 0 as its value. A special case is that of statements about the present, having to do with immediate consequences. Here, relevant options lie one step ahead of the present moment (dt, not n•dt), and to be capable of selection they must have *some* possibility already established in the present ($\neq 0$). I cannot, for example, jump off the Verrazano Narrows Bridge at 4:16 p.m. when I am now at 4:15 typing in New Haven! Thus the first and second propositions say that present and future statements will become definite, the former one moment hence, the latter at some undetermined but future time. These conditions formalize time as a progressive modal transformation, and suggest the interesting question of what sorts of entities behave properly when we treat them as having equal time increments (dt).

There are clearly some series that do not lend themselves to suitable interpretations of passage. For example, take the series of natural numbers as a typical case of any serially ordered set of actual entities. (We could also represent such a series as points on a line, emphasizing their mutual connection and introducing the spatial concepts of distance and direction.) Now, clearly, I can pay attention to any element I want, and choose any one as present, while thinking those beyond it come before, moving thus from possible to actual in my thought. But equally clearly, I believe, that change is only in my thought: the points and numbers are all actual, whether I focus on all or one of them or none. By my definition, a serial order of actual entities cannot exist in or as a time that passes. This is not surprising—such an actual serial order is what we discover time really is when we penetrate a reality behind time as it appears. To understand time in this way, we identify it with some set of related actual entities for each element of which the law of identity holds in its strictest form; this is what spatializes time, freezes and stops it.

For cycles that repeat, there are two distinct cases. If the cycles are numerically distinct for each recurrence, then in fact they form a linear series that qualifies as a calendar or clock variety of passing time. But suppose the other case, that there is no way to treat, refer to, or recognize the recurring cycle in question as numerically distinct. (This seems to be the case for the Platonic Great Year, and the notion finds echoes in modern cosmology and ancient astronomy.) In this case, as Aristotle remarked, "the same term is both antecedent and consequent," hence is both past and future relative to any other term. Events in such a numerically single cycle are a second case that does not satisfy the passage conditions defined above.[5]

By taking away its numerical self-identity, the closed pure cycle of the second case is transformed into an epicyclic form. Such epicycles are the patterns of the various species' life-cycles in Aristotle's natural philosophy. This could, indeed, be recognized as a time that passes, but the Platonist and Aristotelian would like to identify the epicycle illicitly with non-passing pure cyclic time. Aristotle does this when he argues that we have necessary knowledge of the identical recurring forms in natural cycles. But we have since found empirically (the theory of evolution is the most spectacular result of this finding) that their numerical difference also introduces a possibility of deviation into recurrences of epicycles which are future to a given "now" (t0). A universe with constant modal identity among all its subordinate cycles should not admit of even epicyclic passing time.[6] And, in agreement with Aristotle in other passages (e.g., *Physics* II.2), I take it to be an empirical fact that we live in a world where time either does, or does seem to, pass.[7]

In the formulas (1)–(3), the symbol dt, standing for some equal increment of passage, is crucial in each formula. But this purely formal symbol does not in itself give any hint of the range of dt, nor tell us what such equal increments of passage are. Four candidates are suggested by the fact that there are four distinct analyses of time in Western philosophy. They are: (1) time as a space-like extended dimension, or as an actual series; (2) time as recurrent periodic motion; (3) time as progressive maturity or age; and (4) time as a distention of the soul, awareness of the sequences of states and events that make up our subjective experience.[8] These four form a hierarchy, and science, philosophy, even common sense, constantly try to reduce the lower levels to the higher.[9] Thus we measure our ages by calendars and clocks, treating the latter as marking out distances in an abstract mathematical space. Our subjective time, with its peculiar fits, starts, ebbs and flows, we correct against an average aging or functioning rate, then reduce this to calendar and clock. The end of this reduction lies in the shift from epicycle to pure cycle in the Platonic hierarchy.

Of these four classical definitons of time, the first (pure series) clearly is not time that passes at all. The second (the impure epicycle) divides into two cases, one of which does not fall in our field of investigation, but the other of which does. It is now time to explore the third notion of time: time construed as increments of growth, or maturity, or age. In the maturing of people and animals, the progressive actualization of powers, organic structures, and functions, we find a series perfectly suitable as values of dt. "Things age as time passes" is quite a sensible statement.[10]

Perhaps it does not seem sensible to treat equal increments of maturity as a time because clock-and-calendar public time ought to be the only interpretation for dt. The suggestion that increments of maturity may be *equal* is rejected when it turns out that, wherever we define and compare them, they are *unequal* measured by chronometer. But this only happens when we are thinking about it. And, whereas there is an elimination of passage from clock and calendar time language, the exact opposite is built into the semantics of our ordinary time-as-maturity vocabulary. Growth time and clock time can never coincide for successive stretches, because if we have a constant (clock rate) input of increments—of nutrition, of information, of form—more and more are needed for transformations as an organism grows older. To take an illustration from Aristotle, a child on the second day of its life doubles the amount of experience it had by the end of its first day. The intellectually mature Aristotelian, aged 49, adds in the first day of his 50th year a new increment of experience equal to 1/17,895th of that he has already had. To double his experience he would have to live well beyond any historically recorded human life-span.

The irreversible process of living is much more obviously a time that passes than the repetitive epicyclic advance of calendar and clock. As far as these latter go, it seems quite arbitrary that we are located just *now* in their easily spatialized scheme. It really may not matter to the physical sciences whether the now (t0) cuts between modally different past fact and future possibility, or only discriminates events into a "now" and "not now," as they are divided by the revolving present of a pure cycle. But unlike that abstract time of physics, our lives are always being lived in an absolute *now* which cuts apart what we have been and done from what we may become and do. Our time alive on earth is finite, with sharp limits; we can anticipate its coming to an end. And it has an evident one-directionality: we can feel our bodies building up, then running down.[11]

When we look at our ways of talking, at our customs, at our law, we find that long experience has marked out the approximately equal increments of human life-time. The most significant usage here is our description of people as about the same age. We do not say this of a two-year-old and a four-year-old, but nearly always say it about two people aged fifty-two and fifty-four. Funded observation has, in a general way, correlated increments of maturity with periods of calendar time. The result is the familiar magic number, seven, in our social structure.

At 7, children can begin to be conscious of sin, according to theologians; it is custom to pay half price for admissions and fares; they start grade 1 in school.

At 14 (about), the half fare changes to full. This is the young adult stage: we break education here, between the seven grades of elementary school and high school. But not until another 7 years have passed do we recognize fully adult maturity; except that somewhere about here the pediatrician is exchanged for a physician.

At 21, children have grown up; they can own property, marry without their parents' consent, vote in elections; they can no longer be tried by juvenile courts. Formal education of a non-specialist kind ends about here.

At 28, a good deal happens; but with no special legal recognition.

At 35, a person is middle-aged (according to others still in their teens or twenties); he or she is now eligible for the office of President of the United States; according to Aristotle, he (not she) is now in his physical prime. (Aristotle, does not say how he measures this.)

At 42, again, much may happen; but there is no special recognition of this.

At 49, man reaches his full intellectual maturity, according to Aristotle when he was about 49. But society takes no special cognizance of this fact.

At 56, once more, however much happens, this is not marked off as an increment by our language or law.

At 63, it is about time to retire. (No longer; by federal law, this age is not 9 x 7, but 10 x 7.)

At 70, a human life has reached its normal span of threescore years and ten; cases of continued mental growth are exceptions after this point.

(Alternative calculations, however [Plato this time], fixed the optimum human life span at 98 ± 2.)

We are amused by the colloquial inexactness and primitive geomancy of this inherited scheme, and with some justification. And yet, the equal increments of maturity do seem to be pretty well marked off. But, as we said above, these increments do not correspond to equal periods measured by the calendar. In fact, their calendar lengths give the series:

$$dt \text{ (calendar)} = 7, \ 14, \ 21, \ 28, \ 35.$$

We can learn a good deal more about this scale by noticing how we use such phrases as "don't be childish," "he's old for his years," or "he's young for his age."

Of course, medical science and psychology have more precise studies of growth and physiological aging, as do actuaries and statisticians. There remain some major problems to be solved, however, before their work and the sort of pragmatic scale discussed just above can be brought into precise connection. But our pragmatic observation already shows us that there is an error involved in our instinctive habit of correlating our own average rates of work, attention, imagination, with some public clock, and then assuming that for everyone else there will be just this same correlation. An average or normal subjective time rate changes with organic age.[12]

But an even more difficult and interesting question is that of determining the remnants of pure abstract form of the elusive passing time of variable—not average—individual subjective rates of thinking or experience rates. Such subjective time, in its actual, not merely average, flow adds yet a new degree of instability, unreality, and non-being to the pure form of time with which we began. Times such as clock time, growth time, even as some average rate of experience, have enough fundamental continuity and regularity in their flow so that they can be given fairly simple formalization and measure. But variable subjective time escapes regularity: its increments violate conditions of even flow, and we discover that they stretch and shrink wildly as correlated with age and clock.

There is still, however, an application of the time-passes formula which makes it possible to talk to our fluid inner life as time, and a time that passes. Taking as model E. M. Berkeley's "Algebra of States and Events," the divisions of our experience as noticed and remembered mark off the increments of a subjective time.[13] We all find that we remember experiences in terms of successive happenings and continued activities. I remember a picnic—it is a unified item; then, after that, there was a boat ride; then we rested while we watched a sunset. My memory has fixed certain points as points of change between one remembered unit and another. These points of change will be interpreted as events interrupting the relatively unified states that are the [$dt(s)$] increments in my memory. An absolutely even intensity of subjective sensation or ideation input is uneventful and usually remembered as undivided. Thus a five-hour wait in the Muskegon bus terminal, spent in reading essays on the philosophy of mind, is one item in my memory of a recent trip; fifty minutes by car, looking for the right dirt road to Camp Miniwanca, is at least five items.

In connection with motion, it is interesting that it is not simply changes in velocity (which are changes in input intensity) that mark off the states we remember as units of experience. We adapt quickly to uniform acceleration, and find this, until it is interrupted, uneventful. An accelerating car; a sled ride down the hill; the rise to a crescendo in music; all of these are single items. What we do notice is discontinuity in acceleration. (With some few spectacular exceptions where there is a repeating rhythmic pattern to the change, as in the rocking chair.) Representing the passage of subjective time by states and events, the state is an experience with some continuity in its intensity, the event an interruption. Using I for "input rate," "intensity," or whatever name best suits experience as we live through it, Berkeley's model suggests a rather strange, but plausible, formula for defining the states and events of subjective time.

This is a definition of state and event: $\text{s} = \text{df } dI/dt = \text{k};$
$$\text{e} = \text{df } dI/dt \neq \text{k}$$
(dI/dt is the derivative of input with respect to clock time; k is a constant.) But this does not account for the unity we feel in cases of uniform acceleration, nor for the fact that there can be changes within an experience which is still remembered as an undivided whole. The same considerations show the unsuitability of defining events by a second derivative of input over time. For rates of change of velocity of

input do not seem eventful in the cases where the change of rate is uniform—which is exactly what we mean by uniform acceleration. The right definition is the one below:

$$s = \mathrm{df}\, d\mathrm{I}^3/d^3\mathrm{t} = k$$
$$e = \mathrm{df}\, d\mathrm{I}^3/d^3\mathrm{t} \neq k.$$

This simply says that it is discontinuities of acceleration of any input, I, that we notice as the events that divide states. This is borne out by navy research on motion sickness: what causes this is not the regular ship motions of pitch, toss, and roll, but the choppy ones, yaw, heave, surge, and sway.[14]

If we think of experience as an intensity input curve, a sine function with crests at A, C, E and troughs at B, D, F, all six could be events dividing states, since all six are changes of the rate of acceleration. There is, however, a radical difference in the way the two sets divide; and we find that some people habitually choose the set A, C, E, not noticing B, D, F, while others remember experience as divided at B, D, F, without noticing the available alternative division at A, C, E. The divisions at A, C, E mark *completions*; and when these alone structure experience, we have a perfective subjective time sense: things are always seen as fixed, achieved, and over. The divisions at B, D, F, on the other hand, mark *inceptions*: and, where these are the only events used to structure experience, the result is a time-sense that is inceptive.[15] (It seems to me that ordinary language usually takes the side of the perfective time-sense. This way plays things safe, but it is uncreative. The progressive and present eternal tenses have also found their way into some of the languages we use; but the inceptive standpoint seems to have been suppressed. The best inceptive English I can think of is the American dialectal "fixin' to do." Aristotle noted in his *Rhetoric* that "old men think of life as all past, mature men as present, young men as all future." Perhaps the language of a tribe has always been stabilized by an Academy of old men?)

In any case, with time defined as an experienced state and event sequence we have come almost as far as we can from the serially ordered set of extended equal increments with which we began. There, all temporally equal items were congruent in extension in a quasi-spatial field; here, we do well to find the few traces of that tidy order that survive in spite of differential bending, stretching, and shrinking.

This lack of tidiness is in part due to the simultaneous operation, in subjective time, of so many superimposed foreground and background series with differing content and order.

This is, however, a world of story and shadow we are exploring, and there are radical private differences that appear within the rough formal similarity of the state-event-state-event pattern. The set of these discussed above is a difference in the noticing of tenses or aspects of the experiences we remember. This psychological noticing takes on much more practical importance by virtue of *anticipation*, the counterpart of memory. Anticipation has to do with an ordered relation of a present to some future experience. It has two important properties. First, in its stronger intensities, anticipation selects a future event as the next significant cut in one's experience. This has the effect of smoothing out and blocking any potential subordinate events between the present and this anticipated goal. Waiting is the extreme case here: we either become irritated at the monotony, or shift our thoughts into neutral gear, escaping a distention of soul which is uncomfortable.

The second property of anticipation is that the same selective tense structure can operate here that operates in what we *remember* and what we *notice*. On my screen of imagination, I may outline my future in perfective patterns, anticipating a series of things as they will be when they are complete—and so determinate and past. This has the awkward effect of making me fail to recognize that I have reached the goal I anticipated until that goal matches my image in full concrete detail; in other words, until my action is over. This device, associating anticipated events with the sort of closure peculiar to remembered states, goes counter to the objective character of a passing time, and leaves its possessor always looking backward even when he or she stands ahead of the present in his or her imagination. This way of viewing experience is what Bergson and others have criticized as assuming future possibilities as already having the determinate actuality that they will only have when they are not future.[16] But this frame is the construction of a human agent, and neither selective attention nor absent-mindedness can change the fact that every such agent really is immersed in the objective passage of both cosmic and organic time.

This analysis shows, as an incidental consequence, that we can create more subjective time for ourselves per given unit of clock time and given organic age. Anticipation, waiting, and similar states of future orientation do not rule out the possibility of noticing something eventful or new before reaching some exact envisioned goal. To illustrate the point, let me fall back on a simple pastoral example I first used in 1967. Then, and now, I often go from my office to the Sterling Memorial Library. On a day when I am in a hurry, the four-minute concentrated walk down High Street counts as just one increment of experience, a locomotion from here to there. But on another day, I may set out more at leisure psychologically, though at the same pace. Then I notice the sculptured head of Socrates on the library roof; a plump squirrel racing north along a wall; a weather-vane owl turning atop Berkeley College; a southbound student who calls, in passing, that the library still lacks Spiegelberg's book on Socrates. And so this second four-minute trip—with weather vane, Socrates, squirrel, student—has held four increments of experience, of modest adventure, in its fixed wristwatch time. This is the sort of thing I have in mind when I say that concrete noticing can create more subjective time for ourselves.

One might suppose—as I think most of us do unconsciously suppose—that since the time of the cyclic type is both the public time we regulate our lives by and the exact time of the sciences, common sense and ordinary language would have a good deal to tell us about it. But they do not; and closer reflection shows that they do not for a very good reason. A human language that always took an absolute, objective "now" as its standpoint would have to keep its tenses oriented to the single, objective, past, present, and future which that "now" defines. But inquiry, storytelling, planning, and imagination all involve a shift between the "now" which their statements assume as reference point and the unique now which is the objective present of the speaker or reader. If I am to appreciate history, for example, I must have an historical present orientation: that is, I must be able to describe and imagine myself in a past situation with that past having the modal character it had when it was present. And in my planning, a kind of future perfect tense, though it may be a metaphysical absurdity, is an absolute practical necessity.[17] One needs this to set out means-end sequences and indicate what at each stage will and will not still be open to reconsideration and control.

The upshot of this is that whether a given language uses a straight tense or an aspect system for the time component of its verbs, it is usually impossible to tell whether the *actual now* of the speaker matches the *linguistic now* of his statements. I can describe the trial of Socrates as though I were present, and discuss tomorrow's picnic as though it were already over and a fact in the past. This open frame is, I believe, essential to human cooperation and survival; but it is fatal in any attempt to understand and describe passage in ordinary language. The different linguistic roles allow me to treat present, future, and past with any degree of distance and direction I choose; this posits a static series of entities or events preserving their identities quite indifferent to the passage of time.[18]

The syntax of language, in other words, is an elastic gossamer net. It has no correlation with objective sequence and structure; it serves primarily, so far as time is concerned, to permit us to act out various subjective scenarios. Thus, while every sentence contains its own "now" as its internal standpoint, and this can be taken as a modal cut between a past and future, any standpoint can be assumed as t0. Language, when it comes to time, allows each sentence to be its own imaginary world and does not impose even subjective time. For subjective time conserves chronological order, giving its state-event patterns a privileged direction. Linguistic time does not. For example, as a novelist writing about the trial of Socrates, I can write: "Tomorrow is the crucial day!" As an actor, dramatizing Plato's *Apology*, I can introduce my part: "Now, I stand before you, a jury of Athenians." As historian, I say: "There is no doubt that the trial of Socrate took place in 399 B.C." Here, finally, it is only within a given arbitrary context that one can find any forms of passage. And, naturally enough, we try to correct this by semantic rather than syntactic correlations, which anchor our sentences to some objective temporal orientation (what we mean to say, when we make an assertion, whether we are reporting or imagining).

Finally, at the very edge of pure unreality, we come upon time as a sheer succession of isolated moments or static spatial states.[19] Such flashing, evanescent points and lines fall outside of any passing time order, just as does the numerically identical recurring cycle on its higher level of reality. Since the postulated moments have no internal connection, both induction and causality are unaccountable. So also are order and succession. We must recognize continuity, and memory with imagination, to have a field in which such moments can be related in a sequential order. The investigation has come full circle: for moments placed in this extended field, numbered as though they were determinate, recapture the identification of time with the number series with which our descent began. The main difference is that our moments now lack the internal relatedness which gave points on a line and integers in series a non-arbitrary order.[20]

My conclusion is what a Platonist would expect. On each level, the pure formal order is further modified. With cyclic time, it moves from the one-mode extended number series to a recurring cycle that is bi-modal; with passing time it becomes tri-modal and one-directional; until, finally, on the level of language, an arbitrary "now" divides the non-uniform and private subjective states and events which serve as its measure.

To understand any given level we contrast it to a higher level of the hierarchy. Experience or subjective time makes sense when contrasted with growth and public time; public time is an asymmetrical modification of pure cyclic time; cyclic time requires an atemporal, extended background of eternity for its comprehension. I have tried to indicate how the unchanging form of time mixes with non-being to produce the several imperfect series in which time passes, series that our reason cannot help rejecting as unreal. Our own existence, immersed in becoming, shares this same admixture of unreality. This descent to Plato's cave is the only way for us to understand the peculiar nature of physical, biological, psychological, and most Protean of all, linguistic time.

CHAPTER SIX
On Teaching and Learning:
What It Is Like to Learn

This chapter and Chapter 7 are concerned with some matters of precision in considering the technical, discipline phase of education. They are written from the standpoint of the teacher or administrator who must select materials, plan classes, design curricula, and meet the problems of motivation and evaluation.

Let me begin with a remark about language: the terms "teaching" and "learning" cover a wide range of experience, and vary widely depending on the subject matter being taught or learned. Whitehead was always aware of this; to illustrate his own notions, he cited poets, commended attention to classical technology, drew lessons from history, and commented on impressionism in painting. But still he was firmly in the Platonic tradition when he cited paradigm cases of learning. His examples are formal and visual: intellectual discipline is illustrated by references to mathematics (with a large component of geometry); aesthetic appreciation is illustrated by ordinary and special visual experiences. These two types of illustration apply excellently to the discipline phases of mathematics, logic, classical language study, and (perhaps) appreciation of graphic art. They apply less well to other kinds of learning. For example, history and civics do not have the precise problems and solutions that grammar and logic do; and problems here—unlike the solitary ones of the mathematician—are often best solved by group collaboration. Again, in the aesthetic domain, appreciation requires more than simply presentaton. It requires both some indication, by a critic or teacher, of properties that contribute to aesthetic interest, and concurrent creative work by the student himself or herself. (It is a great aid to perceiving the beauty of a sonnet to have tried to write some of them.)

The consequence of this is that an outline treatment of what is common to all subject matters in the precision phase of education must be abstract and very general, indeed much more so than Whitehead himself suggested. It is necessary to distinguish and design proper disciplines for situations of different types. Probability theory, not the absolute proof of formal logic, is appropriate to propaganda analysis and rules of evidence. As Aristotle said, it is equally inappropriate to accept mere probabilities from a mathematician and to demand rigorous proofs from a politician.

One thing I have sometimes done to make this point to my students is to set up a sort of laboratory: a set of exercises with examples of contrasting kinds of learning. I will describe some of these case studies. The themes of discipline and abstraction can be treated too abstractly, imposing a single type of case, a paradigm, on all subject matter. While it is easy to get students and teachers to agree to all this in the abstract, they do not concretely believe it. So there is some point in inventing the learning laboratory that picks out extreme kinds of learning experiences in order to focus on the different feeling of different inquiries and problems, thereby making this abstract reasoning about learning persuasive by virtue of first-hand encounters. In the spring of 1972, I turned my office into a small-scale learning laboratory for a group of graduate students. The instruction sheet began:

LABORATORY: LEARNING

Purpose of experiment: to see what it feels like subjectively to learn with and about different kinds of materials and problems.

When one learns something, there is a kind of satisfaction, of completeness, to the experience. Plato's model of learning is insight [we had studied the *Meno* and *Republic* III, VI, VII], Aristotle's is study of ordered specimens [we had worked with *Physics* II and the *Poetics* in this connection]. With Dewey and Whitehead, we may find still other models [as also with Skinner and Neill].

Experiments: Go around the office to the left; directions for each of five case studies in types of learning have been set up. Keep in mind the purpose of this experiment, and the possibility that the result may be negative—i.e., that even in this specially arranged case, all learning experiences may be subjectively the same.

I. Learning as formal insight. [A small three-dimensional two-piece plastic puzzle on a table.] Fit the two pieces together to make a pyramid with a square base. Any questions about whether you have solved the problem? Anything left over? [Obviously, one could do this with any mathematical example; the familiar two-dimensional dissections of a square, or the arithmetical theorem to be proven that the difference of a number written normally and written with its digits reversed is always a multiple of nine, and so on.]

Now, the interesting thing about this first kind of learning is its *total closure*, and its dependence on insight that comes suddenly. In the background, for mathematical examples, there is also a feeling of inevitability: even if we do not work out a proof, we have a feeling that we could show—given the starting data—that the solution is necessarily right. But, in addition to these feelings of closure, insight, and logical inevitability, formalist type-specimen learning situations are *anti-social*. General conversation, special apparatus, and so on, only get in the way of the person looking for a proof. By and large, the ideas about proper conditions for study in the West have been generalizations from this anti-social property of the formalist learning model.

The second case study tried to bring out learning as empirical inquiry—both as taxonomic work with ideas, and as information acquired by handling standard artifacts.

II. Learning as empirical inquiry. (In two parts.)

1. Get an ancient coin from the collection. How much can you tell from looking at it about the culture that produced it? What additional information would you need to be sure, for example, that you do not have a reflection of a matriarchal society rather than one with female deities? [A set of three Athenian tetradrachmae, with the head of Athena on one side, her owl, an olive-leaf and lettering on the other, were used for this exploration.]

2. Read the "Coins and Greek Philosophy" captions. Does having the actual coins make a difference to your feeling about Plato's metaphor of physical reality as minted space?

First Coin Caption:

There are a number of reasons for looking at Greek coins at the time one is studying Greek philosophy. For one thing, here is tangible evidence that the Greeks were real, not just names in our textbook; and some of the cultural associations of the coins (what they could buy, or be used for) reinforce the fact that the makers and users of these tangible objects were human beings like ourselves—purchasers of books, onions, boat tickets, and de luxe copies of manuscripts. A second reason is that these coins show the sort of aesthetic excellence we have in mind when we say the Greeks had a sort of absolute pitch in their sense of form and beauty; no coins as beautifully designed as these have been made since; and it seemed reasonable to commission the finest engravers to cut dies for these utilitarian items. The most important reason is the way in which these coins reflect a Greek idea of the relevance of the ideal to the actual: it is the ideal type which gives the (carefully weighed, but otherwise roughly shaped) lump of silver its identity as an Athenian tetradrachma. Apparently, the Greek could see so clearly what the design was trying to be ideally, that there were no complaints about the sloppy striking techniques of the mint; if Athena's nose did not get on the coin, you could see exactly where it should be. But the poor technique and massive silver blanks also suggest that there was an inexact fit of ideal and actual; the medium had a certain recalcitrance to hold form.

Other captions suggested other ways that a study of ancient coins could illustrate themes in the history of ideas. For example, a shift in artistic vision is illustrated by three silver tetradrachmas: the first is pure Hellenic, an idealized Alexander portrayed as Herakles; the second moved one step toward realism with a plumper, more human (yet still idealized) Lysimachus as Herakles—looking as though he were trying to capture the expression of the Alexander coin; the third is several centuries later, Ptolemy V of Egypt (ca. 210–180 B.C.) costumed as Zeus, but a Zeus whose curved nose and chin nearly met, like a crescent moon or like the actual features of Ptolemy. The significance of Plato's comparison of physical objects to things minted out of space was the topic of a second caption: the contrast between the heavy, individually weighed and struck, ancient silver pieces and modern American mass-produced token currency (for example, silver dimes) can change the young philosopher's appreciation of Plato's simile.

The laboratory continued with a pair of questions: "Where would you go to get a solution to the first of these problems? What does "solution" mean here? Different from the pyramid puzzle?" In the first place, it is clear that the answers are *inexhaustible*. One can go on building and testing hypotheses about facets of the culture all the way from their metallurgy to their dependence on olive oil for vitamins. There is no solution! In the second place, it is clear that aids and apparatus are required. I provided a lens; but several students would also have liked some kind of balance, a larger selection of samples for comparison, an analysis of the metal, and so on. In the third place, work on a problem of this kind is radically *social*—the number of ideas advanced and tested, and the amount of interest in the advancing and testing, were so much greater when three or four students were working on this at once, that I brought in a student assistant to begin shared inquiry whenever there was only one student there in the office. I also included in this experiement a pair of books about classical coins as a quiet reminder that empirical inquiry of this kind could also go on in a museum or library.

My third experiment was somewhat impure. It was a novelty jug both difficult to classify in function and tricky to analyze in operation. I thought of it mainly as a taxonomic problem at first, but my students treated it as a challenge to atomistic technological analysis.

III. Learning as empirical taxonomy.

This is very like II. In the office bathroom is a small jug-like artifact. [There was also a rubber lab apron.] Nothing has ever been written about it except for a note in one guidebook to Samos that amusing things (*maskares barthakies*) are still made from an ancient design by the potters of the town of Mavratzay. What is it; how does it work; can you find out how to drink wine from the spout without getting splashed?

This was an artifact my science students admired: a hollow handle with a single hole could be used as a drinking straw when the hole was covered to draw wine from deep in the pitcher. The upper part was punched full of holes, so that any attempt to drink by tilting was sure to be unsuccessful. I thought this fell somewhere between the total closure of the formalist material and the relative lack of it of the historical artifacts.

As a fourth dimension, I wanted an exercise in aesthetic sensitivity or creativity. This is a peculiarly tricky kind of learning to discuss and include in a theory, although I insisted that it *is* one kind of learning.

IV. Learning as aesthetic insight.

Read the translated poems on the desk. [There were five haiku poems by Bashō in various translations. They appear below as an appendix.] One of them reads: "A solitary crow is perched / upon a leafless bough— / One autumn eve." From Bashō's other paintings, it seems that the toy Steiff mina bird [a plump, black toy bird about three inches long on the desk] is almost a perfect illustration for his crow. Do you learn anything at all from the poems? Take a card [a pile of 3x5 cards were on the desk] and write your own two-line haiku, trying to match the pattern of image-contrast Bashō uses. How does it feel to solve this problem, as compared to the pyramid assembly and artifact identification?

Perhaps his insistence that such a dimension of concreteness be part of any sound educational method was Whitehead's most important contribution to educational theory. (It is different from Dewey's concrete activities: those are better represented by the pitcher or the first exercise with ancient coins.) It has a mixture of open- and closed-boundaries to it that is its own. The intensity involved in composing one's own poem is like mathematical or formalist insight; but the infinity of open possibilities is peculiar to this aesthetic kind of activity. On the other hand, there are some aspects of closure and craft in constructing the poem; and, by and large, a social dimension—we wonder (perhaps only when our poem has been finished) how some other reader will respond to the choice of evocative imagery.

Having set up these paradigms, I still was not sure that justice had been done to the Aristotelian world, or at least to that world in its practical dimension. And I wanted some transition between the interesting but relatively self-enclosed hour or so in my office and the application of ideas outside of it. So as a final item, I set up a problem in quick practical planning.

V. Learning as practical planning and projection.

Look quickly at a book and write a brief paragraph indicating whether it would be useful in school libraries or classes; if so, how would you use it, and where? (BOOKS ON TOP OF BOOKCASE AT FAR LEFT.)

Among the books I included Burstall's *Working Models of Ancient Machines*; D. E. Smith and J. Ginsburg, *Numbers and Numerals*; Henderson's *Introduction to Haiku*; my own *Ancient Greek Gadgets and Machines*; and Seltman's small *A Book of Greek Coins*. My students, by and large, short-changed this last experiment, though they all thought the laboratory had been interesting. But it had also been more rigorous than I expected. While I was out for a twenty-minute lunch break, three young men started around the course; by the time I came back, they had decided the whole thing was rigged as "a deliberate ego-buster"; that there were *no* solutions to the pyramid puzzle or the Samos pitcher! A woman who got the pyramid in four easy seconds stayed for an hour working on the haiku. The sheer data of time, attention, and comment were very interesting. Many students seemed to feel that they were encountering as *actual* something they had not before even entertained as *possible*. I had to use the lure of coffee and the coercion of closing time to disengage some of them—a young literature major from the Ptolemy coin, an ex-science teacher from the Samos jug, an experimental psychology expert from the haiku poetry desk.

My reason for presenting this material in this way was, as I said, that as an abstract argument my theory of discipline tends to be plausible but empty. We agree verbally that there are alternative paradigms; and that each theorist tends to oversell his own, but we do not really feel that "this means me." But if the reader can, in his or her imagination, follow the description of the puzzles and items in my office collection, it may be that some of the concrete meaning and conviction of this general thesis concerning paradigms and education can be communicated. Learning is an ambiguous term; all kinds of it can be fun; and in different situations, we cannot deny that it feels different to learn.

Appendix: Five Haiku by Bashō

I. THE RUINS OF TAKADACHI FORT

Natsugusu ya Tsuwamono domo ga Yume no ato.
> Ah, summer grasses wave!
> The warriors' brave deeds
> Have proved an empty dream!
> —trans. A. Miyamori

II. A CROW ON A BARE BRANCH

Kare-ede ni Karasu no tomari keri Aki no kure.
> A solitary crow is perched
> Upon a leafless bough—
> One autumn eve.
> —trans. A. Miyamori

III. THE OLD POND

Furuike ya Kawazu tobikome Mizu no oto.
> The ancient pond!
> A frong has plunged—
> Splash!
> —trans. A. Miyamori

Compare:
> Into an old pond
> A frog took a sudden plunge,
> Then is heard a splash.
> —trans. I. Nitobe

> Old garden lake!
> The frog thy depth doth seek,
> And sleeping echoes wake.
> —trans. H. Saitō

> An ancient pond!
> The frog leaps in;
> The sound of water.
> —trans. M. Toyoda

82

Into the calm old lake
A frog with flying leap goes plop
  The peaceful hush to break.
        —trans. W. N. Porter

IV. THE MILKY WAY

Ara-umi ya Sado ni yokotō Ama-no-gawa.
  The sea is wild!
  The Milky Way extends
  Far over Sado isle.
        —trans. A. Miyamori

O rough sea! Waves on waves do darkling rise,
The galaxy reaching down where Sado lies.
        —trans. S. Nishimura

A stormy sea—
To Sado Isle reaches
The River of Heaven.
        —a try at trans. by RSB

(N.B. There is a copy of this poem in the poet's hand. If we try to
reproduce emphasis or heaviness typographically, what he wrote was:

WILD SEA—by Sado stretches—RIVER OF HEAVEN)

V. THE QUAILS

Take no me no Ima ya kure nu to Naku uzura.
  The quails are chirping,
    Aware that hawks' eyes
      Are dim now in the dusk.
        —trans. A. Miyamori

CHAPTER SEVEN
On Concrete Seeing

Of all recommendations for education that follow from process philosophy, the most controversial and most difficult to implement, or even to understand, is the insistence that concrete appreciation be given equal importance as facility with abstractions. And, in this context, equal importance implies equal time.

Why this proposal is realistic, we have seen already. In discussing space, the contrast between abrupt and associated hierarchies, which represent abstractions and concrete occasions, is crucial. The actual entities can neither be constructed nor exhaustively described by the addition of sets of abstractions. And in treating sequence, we saw that in the context of larger social patterns, those of civilization and social progress, there is a risk that individuals in a technologically advanced society may see each other only as abstractions. Further, in discussing sequence, we noted that the first phase of concrescense, that of encounter, can be impoverished or over-selective. If the data presented are thin and abstract, there will not be enough energy, or romance, to start off an important sequence of concrescence. If it lacks aesthetic vividness, it will be grasped only as an abstraction; recognized, but not appreciated. For human experience, this means an encounter with something of known name or measure, but not engaged in its own right. Finally, in discussing logic and time, we pointed out that an increased awareness of each increment of experience is the secret of

The section on the aesthetic interest of the removal of form is from "Notes on Art, Aesthetics, and Form," *Par Rapport: A Journal of the Humanities*, I (1978): 23–25. Copyright by Doug Bolling. Reprinted by permission.

longevity, defined as the number of adventures and experiences in a lifetime.

I will go on to argue that history, as well, with its cycles of civilization and advance of religious vision, involves encounters between cultures and their individual representatives. We need, Whitehead says, to have neighbors who will challenge us—but: "we must not expect our neighbors to have all the virtues. It is enough if they are sufficiently different to be interesting." There are two different topics for examination here. The first is the emergence and development of this theme in Whitehead's own writing. That seems to me the best way to discover exactly what his own recommendation meant. The second topic, which I take up first, is the philosophic question of how—apart from anyone's historical suggestions—the recommendation can be carried out. (This will be more tentative and exploratory than any other part of my discussion of metaphysics and education. The reason is that appreciation is the inverse of explanation; so to explain appreciation will certainly require an unfamiliar use of symbolism, to the extent to which it can be done at all. Compare Bergson's use of symbolic language to present a metaphysics, which he defines as the science that dispenses with symbols.)

In the first place, to appreciate something in its own right we do not think of it either as a type specimen or commodity or tool. A proper display case or frame encourages appreciation; for, a frame is an effective pragmatic insulator: we are free to contemplate its content, but not to use it. (In fact, sometimes a frame has another interesting effect: we feel we are in two places at once, aware of our world, but also feeling ourselves in the other system of society, space, and time that we see framed. Whitehead's characterization of the scene through a train window as an intuition of a time system non-cogredient with our own has extraordinary suggestiveness for film and literary criticism.)

Now, the frame is a taxonomic insulator as well as a pragmatic one. It interposes a difference between abstract type and an actual entity, exactly this thing, that it encloses. In this role, it therefore acts as an indicator. But it is possible to understand the frame, mistakenly, as an invitation to apply categories of art history and art appreciation to its content. This misunderstanding would make the frame behave like another variety of abstraction operator, not indicator. Of course, there is a value to locating art in terms of period, influence, school, and style. But Whitehead was justifiably doubtful about art appreciation approaches which simply replace one set of abstract classifications with another. It is not *a* pink house in Bloomington, Illinois, that is the subject of the framed picture in my living room, it is *this* pink house—not just in Bloomington, but within a larger midwestern context, and within it at exactly this place and at exactly this season and time of day. (The painting is "Old Pink House in Bloomington, Illinois," by Vincent Paul Quinn, 1938.)

I think that looking at things as framed, the frame functioning as pragmatic insulator and indicator, is an essential start toward learning concrete appreciation. (There are persons who have no need to learn this because they naturally see things concretely; this discussion does not apply to them; we do better to learn *from* them.) This marvelous seeing by a bracketing that cuts out any impulse to classify or manipulate offers new interest and reveals new vividness and beauty in unexpected places.

This mention of the unexpected suggests another way of eliciting concrete seeing. When we become completely familiar with ordinary things of a given size, or medium, or function, we tend to ignore anything interesting about them. (Aristotle remarks that we think of the form of man as naturally and inseparably tied to a certain scale, and to a medium of flesh and bone because we have never seen that form in a radically different scale or matter. But in fact, part of the interest of classical sculpture comes—and came—from recognizing the human shape—if not its vital essence—in the medium of stone, and from the shifts in size from primitive colossal scale to classical statues only moderately larger than ourselves.) Andy Warhol's outsized cans of Campbell's soup come to mind; or the Shopping International Catalogue item, a brass desk-top-sized oil well pump. (The brass—a change of medium—is important here, because the real pump, dirty and oil-coated, is so uninterestingly grungy.) Of course, we can look at everyday scenes—small town main streets, factories, refineries—as aesthetically interesting. This is an exercise in the recognition of abstract pattern, hidden beneath the everyday construction. "The hidden harmony is best," wrote Heraclitus; and our artistic resonance to docks, oil refineries, and isolated farmhouses is a recognition of this hidden harmony. And we can hope that our recognition of disharmony will increase too. Plato thought that his citizens, brought up in familiarity with beauty, would always greet her as a friend, but turn away from what is ugly.

At a later stage, artist and audience may feel that a frame is a handicap: it holds our interest artificially, at the expense of the continuity with wider reality which gives an art work importance. This has led to unframing, for example, in such a recent work of art as the life-sized dummy holding a wrapped lunch and seated on a bench with a clear view of the Old Masters in the Yale Art Gallery. But one must first recognize the distancing effect of a frame before the work without or beyond that distance is perceived in full aesthetic vividness. One point that the work of recent artists has underscored is that the artist's aim may not be the creation of beauty in its 19th-century sense but the presentation of new aesthetic interest. Of the two categories, the latter is considerably wider than the former. This becomes particularly clear when we recognize the horrifying or revolting as aesthetically interesting. These certainly have vividness, if not final satisfaction; and Madame Tussaud's Waxworks remains, along with the Tate Gallery, one of the touristic landmarks of London. The Roman Circus, while it disgusted such men of refined taste as Cicero, did well at the box office. And frozen animal kidneys in a refrigerator trailer were the centerpiece of a pop-art show in Manhattan in 1974.

Sometimes sensible ideas and comfortable assumptions that have had a long and useful history cease to apply or need redesign. We must then, in spite of our reluctance, let some of them go. Twentieth-century fine arts offer an interesting case study. What our artists are making and exhibiting, or directing attention to without exhibiting, is a set of events and objects that represent an unfamiliar domain. Their works no longer fit with the concept of the beautiful that dominated fine art in the latter half of the 19th and the first half of the 20th century. Their work suggests—to a watching metaphysician, at any rate—that there is an intuitive, non-reflective readjustment underway in their interest in and valuation of matter and form.

The entrance of form into space and time is always transitory. Therefore, its emergence and disappearance always complement one another. Artists and their critics in the past have celebrated the cre-

ative advent of form, its domination of the medium, but have over-
looked the other side of the symmetrical process, the release of form
from media. This is perhaps quite natural; there are strong psychological grounds for preferring structure to existence. We naturally try
to persuade ourselves that the moment or direction we prefer is the
right, or real, or relevant one by refusing to pay attention to its
balancing contrary. There is a natural human appetite for form: for its
recognition, creation, and contemplation. We take special pleasure in
the vision of strict formal order behind or beneath the surface of the
everyday and familiar, or the eccentric and disorderly. "The hidden
harmony is best," wrote Heraclitus, but even he values the harmony.
Nevertheless, this appetite for order can be sated. By the turn of the
twentieth century, the triumph of form over a recalcitrant medium was
no longer so much a victory, as a total unopposed stamping-press
domination. A contemporary silver quarter no longer has the grace of
form of an ancient Athenian drachma; but neither has it any idiosyncrasies, any intrusiveness of the medium, that suggest that its striking
by the mint was an aesthetic victory. As the twentieth century moves
forward, structural steel skyscraper, concrete superhighway, detailed
bureaucratic regulation of lives and their style, and repetitive technology combine to surround the observer with too much form—both
overt and hidden. This saturation inspires claustrophobia because
forms do have—though I cannot imagine in what way they get it—a
conservative territoriality: once they are embedded in space and time,
they are most reluctant to let go. Aristotle, trying to discover the final
causes of society in his *Politics*, noted this fact: social institutions,
though they are artificial formal structures, still act to insure their own
preservation, and can be dislodged only by revolution. The same thing
is true of the artificial formal structures of roads, telephone
communication lines, customs of cookery, posed photographs of
politicians, and vicarious recreation.
  Resentment of a world wherein too much and too stubborn form
violates proper balance naturally generates a kill-the-umpire interest
in contemplating ways in which forms are moved off the scene,
liberating us from their iron-cage domination. Exactly this shift of
metaphysical evaluation of form seems to explain esome of the things
our contemporary fine artists are doing, things which almost totally

elude such classical formulas as magnitude and order, unity in variety, or truth and symmetry. While there has been a gradual drift in this direction since Plotinus, the turn of our own century has witnessed a surprising, discontinuous leap.

How are tyrannous forms removed, to give us breathing space and more room? One way is to pulverize their space-time incarnations with a wrecking crane, swinging a gigantic iron ball. The demise of the Waldorf Cafeteria, a rather worn out brick structure of unhappy culinary memory, was an aesthetic event: spectators stood entranced watching this at the corner of High and Chapel Streets, quite oblivious to the fact that ten feet away a door to the Yale Art Gallery led to an acreage of Old Masters. The marvelous art work of Tangluey, his machine entitled "Salute to Manhattan," was a player piano that sawed itself in two and burst into fire, well deserving the Courtyard showing it was given at the New York Museum of Modern Art; another interesting demonstration. Embodied forms can be removed: they can be fragmented, compacted, chipped, and incinerated; indeed, they can be given every topologically possible spatial, temporal, and qualitative deformation. And it is aesthetically interesting to see processes that are the converse of the traditional domination of medium by form, creative emergence, *évolution créatrice*. Along the same line, we might expect to find a new interest in the anti-formal appearing as renewed attention to the pure, unposed matter or medium in its stand over against conformity, and in random presentation which, in its unpredictability, falls outside standard patterns of reiteration and sequence. Thus a piano composition of twelve bars of silence, or a uniform silvered glass reflecting surface, may appear before us offering itself as a valuable metaphysical insight embodied in fine art.

A further step in this same direction is seen as some contemporary art tries to unframe itself. Since a frame is, for a work of fine art, a physical or institutional formal insulating device which disconnects its content from any pragmatic use or didactic illustration, we would expect it to be resented as a restraint. The happening which is not a planned procession nor a programmed concert; or the life-sized dummies, mentioned before, who at one time occupied benches and held half-unwrapped lunches in the Yale Art Gallery, adjacent to the former Waldorf Cafeteria, reflect this variation on my theme.

Thus the observer who looks without nostalgia sees that our century is moving toward a new balance in its interest and attention to entrances and exits, field and form. Death, the polar opposite of birth, finds itself a subject for talk shows on TV and for scrutiny by a Society for Thanatology. The temporal opposite of creation, demolition, becomes a central theme for the handling of form in our artistic expression. The pole of matter, once dismissed as proximate to nonbeing, mere bleak potential for form, now appears as a subject of perceptual interest in its own naked neutrality.* In this way, I would suggest, a resentment of the tyranny of ubiquitous form leads to a widening attention to the *exits* that necessarily follow the *entrances* of life, of form, of creativity, even of garish vulgarity, in space and time. And, accordingly, twentieth-century aesthetic theory must extend the range of its inherited classical concept of the beautiful to a much wider and more philosophically profound territory, a new vision of the aesthetically interesting.

One reason for examining this issue of traditional formal beauty and new aesthetic interest is that a pure medium can be interesting, though by conventional criteria it cannot be beautiful and so cannot be an object that can be seen concretely. An encounter with a pure medium at once suggests the metaphysical pole opposed to structure, which must combine with it to yield aesthetic value. We turn, then, to the structure that lies imprisoned in the medium, the form awaiting its release from stone. (Michelangelo, in his sculptures now in the Accademia, gets this effect beautifully by leaving the feet of his figures still unfinished, still in the rough stone, from which the rest of each body has been set free.)

But before we discuss structure and structural analysis, we should examine some other relations basic to full awareness. Separate things in sequence (spatial as well as temporal) may be related in different ways. A sequence of sameness in monotonous—indeed, in the extreme case, it hardly counts as a sequence at all. A sequence of sheer otherness is incoherent, what information theorists call "white thermal noise." A

---

*There is still one exception to this re-balancing of attention to opposite poles; we have not yet quite replaced the traditional attention given to nutrition by equal emphasis on its complementary function, excretion. Between this pair of opposites, our attention and aesthetic interest are still, and I think properly, somewhat one-sided.

sequence or superimposition of mutually neutralizing components is trivial; but too much mutual interaction may end in fission, either literally or psychologically ("mind-blowing!"). For our present purpose, the relations that are most important are those of aesthetic contrast. Contrast differs from monotony, neutralization, fission, and dissonance (used here to include flavors, colors, etc. as well as sounds) . The most simple and sharpest type of contrast is rhythm. Charles Warren, a musicologist and former colleague of mine at Yale, once compared rhythm to the combination of Plato's greatest kinds, the categories of being, same, and other. In fact, one could define a rhythmic sequence as a succession of elements (succession here introduces Plato's fourth category, motion), which exhibit both periodicity and contrast. The elements can be arbitrarily chosen, so long as they remain of the same length relative to other possible choices. So, in a sequence of moments we can let 1 represent a drumbeat of sound, 0 a moment of silence, and use brackets for longer accented groups that can serve as larger elements of sequence. Then $(0,1)' (0,1)' (0,1)' \ldots$ is the simplest rhythmic pattern. Vibrations, of course, consist of rhythmic patterns of this type (often superimposed in complex designs where 1 represents a crest, 0 a trough in a wave pattern).[1] Sharp aesthetic contrast without incoherence is well illustrated by the use of color in the paintings of Josef Albers. By marvelous complementarity, the different contrasts make each color more vivid than it would be alone. In some cases, this technique creates visual images that have rhythmic vibration. Looking for the application of our principle in literature, the maximum high-voltage contrast I have found is in the juxtaposed imagery of classic Japanese haiku poetry. Examples were given in the previous chapter.

An educational theorist thinks at once that we must look for a way to direct attention to this quality of aesthetic contrast in our various sense experiences, and starting with exceptionally vivid cases, transfer this awareness to more subtle ones. As an aid to keeping pedagogical patterns clear, I think we need to develop a logic of aesthetic implication—an *aesthetic* logic to go with current *alethic* and *deontic* schemes. The logic can be based on the relations we have been discussing—sequence, contrast, monotony, incoherence, neutralization, and fission. For example, for any sequence of two elements, p and q, in respect to any property P, p•q equals 1 defines monotony; (pvq)•-(p•q) defines contrast; p•q equivalent p•-p defines neutralization; -(p•p) defines fission. The property table for contrast, where 1 means that an element has a property, 0 that it lacks it, is

p	q	p contrast q
1	1	0
1	0	1
0	1	1
0	0	0

In *The Function of Reason*, 1929, Whitehead wrote that that function is to bring to, and combine in our experience, an awareness of importance and a focus that has interest. The importance comes from a feeling of the connectedness of an object, experience, or idea with a larger—ultimately a cosmic—whole. The interest comes from the sharpness with which a given part displays its definite individuality in contrast to the cosmic background. In Whitehead's own work, a significant development of this theme is indicated by the contrast of two examples used in his discussions of awareness of quality, one in 1911, the other in 1933. In the *Introduction to Mathematics*, he talks about the grey color of the wall of Westminster Abbey. In *Adventures of Ideas*, he talks about the articulation, in an encompassing architectural design, of the individual sculptured figures of the East Portico of the Cathedral of Chartres. In both examples, there is a religious association which lends the experience an enhanced feeling of importance. Note the progression, however, in the characteristics that account for interest. From the pure quality of grey, we come to the heightened contrasts of the individual sculptured figures, which gain in both interest and importance from their integration in the grand architectural sequence and theme of the Portico.

Whitehead is clearly in the Platonic tradition, and in his work visual examples dominate aesthetic illustration. Nevertheless, he also has some very perceptive comments on hearing as our direct access to rhythm, and poetry as expression of cosmological insight. His treatment of Wordsworth and Shelley as respectively grasping the prehensive power of actual occasions and the brittleness and evanescence of eternal objects are cases in point. (However, later, in his conversations with Lucien Price, he said that he had given up reading poetry.) In any case, Platonic tradition or Heraclitean, I think that if we discover a way to teach appreciation in any one medium, we can do it in all others by analogy.

But aesthetic appreciation of art works, natural objects, and various arresting artifacts is not enough. It is crucial that we extend this way of seeing to the different scales appropriate to appreciating a society and a civilization, and to the different dimension appropriate to appreciating another person as an individual. "Since for everything that has come into being, destruction is appointed" (Plato, *Republic* VIII), civilizations, like ourselves, are fated to endure for only a finite time. The law of sequence which follows from the phases of concrescence decrees that every civilization will grow old and fade. But there is no predestined determination of the height to which each will rise. Like learning, the genuine achievement of civilization must, it seems, begin with the energy and wide awareness of intense adventure. (Aesthetic interest is the relevant quality here; intense adventures may be destructive at the time, and unappreciative of finer harmonies.) It must go on to construct new realizations of the aesthetic contrasts to be found in the wide domain of art. And it can end, with vision, in a phase of importance, a harmonized achievement which is peace, and which makes it deserve admiration and satisfaction because of its lasting value. The extreme freedom within the determined framework of rise and decline means that the study of history can never be a science. It also means that there can never be complete agreement among interpreters about either the relative causal importance of different factors or the relative levels of attainment. But such history is, roughly, on our human time scale and so it is particularly interesting for us. It is instructive, too, in showing the way that choices can miss opportunities that are lost forever, or lead to importances and interest gained.

One of the primary values of concrete vision is an appreciation of other individuals. In the Platonic tradition, there is a consensus that there are three kinds of failure in our relations with others: inhumanity, injustice, and insensitivity. Inhumanity is a denial of the essential nature of another human being; it violates the law of contradiction. At least, it does this in a Platonic framework in the following way. By definition, to be human is to be free, rational, and creative; inhumanity is to recognize that an actual occasion, *alpha*, is free, creative, and rational, but still deny that it is human. Injustice is a denial of equality to other human beings. Logically, if *alpha* and *beta* are essentially the same, the one can be substituted for the other in any general context. This is an expression of the idea of an equality of persons in law, and of justice as a kind of fairness. Insensitivity is an absent-minded violation of the laws of concrete attention. It involves lost opportunities for shared interests, experiences, and projects. The realistic fact is that other human beings are, as individuals, aesthetically interesting in their own right. Interest comes more readily at first, perhaps, in those cases of extreme contrast where the other person is from a wholly other culture. Such an alternative type of person is (positively or sometimes negatively) interesting. But a part of the interest in this case comes from the difference of the other person seen as a type, a representative of cultural alternatives. Our objective goes beyond that to an appreciation of someone else as a unique center of thought and feeling, a vivid individual like one's self. (Aristotle uses something like the above set of distinctions in his *Ethics*. God-like or beast-like beings are inhuman, and so for the moralist outside the park. Fellow citizens are persons, and so entitled to impersonal justice and equity. Friends, however, are each another self; they live together, share their studies, and are made more aware of their own existence. Yet if, as Aristotle's discussion suggests, friends are so alike as to be mutual copies, one doubts if increased awareness could possibly result from their predictable feedback and kaleidoscopic symmetrical reflection.)

The basic categories of art appreciation, importance, interest, contrast, and novelty, are also the basic categories of mutual human appreciation. We are important since we share our nature and destiny together; yet we can be manipulated like abstractions since we are separated from our common background, each self-contained through space and time. We are aesthetically interesting since we recognize personal qualities that exhibit contrasts; and our association, despite an intuition that here is another ego like our own, is the occasion of continued novelty and surprise. (I suppose, however, that just as some mundane objects and most abstract entities lend themselves badly to aesthetic appreciation, some personalities lack depth of individuality. One aim of education must be to change whatever causes this effect.)

However, just as novelty with no framework of form, while it may be exciting, is an excitement of incoherence, isolated individuals without some shared framework of goals, social functions, and cultural heritage are not likely to achieve mutual appreciation. Some of the student activists of the 1960s were, I think, misguided in their passionate belief that the United States could have immediate fraternity without a previously implemented structure of legal liberty or of economic equality.

To conclude the present discussion, I believe that its subject, the notion of concrete vision, is the most important contribution process philosophy can offer to the theory of education. It can lead to a new respect for ecology; a new support for artistic creativity; a new vitality of lived experience; and a new degree of personal friendship—among other selves more diverse than Aristotle's multiple reflections of self-identity. We are still a long way from the realization of a full educational system, a good organization of economic production and distribution, or a context of common interests and goals that can increase the number of lifetime units we experience and the intensity per unit of a sense of wonder.

In spite of the criticisms of abstractions, particularly words and numbers, that we have concentrated on, it is still obvious that we must use discussion and conversation to direct attention to what is to be appreciated.[2] There is no necessary long-range destruction of appreciation by the selective attention of critical analysis. There is destruction only when the critical commentary on sources, contrasting components, and sequences is taken to be the end of aesthetic experience; then abstract scholarship is substituted for concrete appreciation. No one should read Kierkegaard's dissertation on irony without then going back to Plato's portraits of Socrates. Dramatic irony, katharsis, and character with a tragic flaw are all structural ingredients of *Oedipus Rex*. But to formalize and separate out those ingredients is mere distraction unless we can then feel new intensity in the concrete texture and evolving action of the play.

CHAPTER EIGHT
Teaching

Introduction

In looking at the teacher, I will offer two case studies and a post-script. The role of the teacher involves transmitting motivation, precise symbolic presentation, and planning for eventual generalization. It also involves being with the student in some shared present time. Socrates, as Plato portrays him in the *Meno*, is a master of motivation. He is able to inspire the most refractory student with a desire to inquire. (It is hard to say whether the teacher in question here is the historic Socrates, or his student, Plato. Since Socrates himself did not write, I will focus on Plato as a master teacher who invents the dialogue form as an extension of Socratic method. The dialogue form gives potential permanence and publicity to Socrates' first-hand, transitory challenges.)

St. Thomas, in speculating how an angel would teach, emphasizes the discipline and precision that belong to the art. The angel can design new, translucent phantasms for the student's imagination; and arrange them in clear deductive order. (Deduction in St. Thomas can be valid by way of any of Aristotle's four causes as principles of logical sequence.) The teacher who does the same need not literally be an angel. The question how, if at all, a superhuman being from another

"Motivation: Plato's Socrates" from "Plato's *Meno* as Form and as Content of Secondary School Courses in Philosophy," *Teaching Philosophy* 1:2 (Fall 1975): 107–115/ Permission for the use of this material has been granted by the Editor of *Teaching Philosophy*. Published for the Teaching Philosophy Association by the Philosophy Documentation Center, Bowling Green, Ohio.

"Precision: St. Thomas' Angel" from "Can Superhuman Beings Teach Us Better than We Can Teach Ourselves?", *Paideia*, forthcoming, Winter, 1981. Copyright by the State University of New York at Buffalo and SUNY College at Brockport.

planetary system, or an artificial intelligence, could teach us is an evident contemporary equivalent. The emphasis here is on the technical moment of the design of signs, patterns, and procedures which give new efficiency to imagination and lead more directly to correct abstraction. Though St. Thomas thinks of teaching mainly in terms of natural language, his notion that the angel may present sensible designs particularly effective in stimulating imagination certainly suggests the use of all sorts of media to get attention and present material clearly.

Finally, a postscript on an adventure of my own argues that at each phase the teacher and student must be together in a creative moment of present time.

Teaching involves four points of technique. It must begin with motivation; it must be as clear and efficient as possible in its moment of skill and precision; it must organize its content in proper sequences for learning; and it must throughout give the student a feeling of being together with the teacher in a shared creative present time. The first of these points, the need for motivation and some ways to achieve it, is given a classical illustration by Plato in the *Meno*. If neither teaching by precept nor by example can make students better, must we conclude that virtue cannot be taught, or may there be some other way?

The second point—the need for skill in symbolic presentation—and the fourth—a kind of immediate transfer of attitude—are two themes of a discussion by St. Thomas Aquinas. In his questions concerning teaching, St. Thomas asks whether a superhuman being (for example, an angel) could teach us better than we can teach ourselves, and if so, how. The relevance of this question to current concern with new media and artificial intelligence is striking. St. Thomas suggests that an angel might be able to present material in symbolism more attention-getting and more easily understood than what human lecturers have devised. (This notion is later applied specifically by Whitehead in an observation on the importance of symbolism in mathematics.) Today this notion suggests new uses for small calculators, motion pictures, television, and foreign-language-translation software.

St. Thomas also suggests that the presence of a superior intelligence would strengthen our own intellectual light. I think this is right; and it has special relevance to the notion of time proper to process philosophy. My tables (see chapter nine) of the eleven ways in which teaching plans can be bad are interesting corollaries. They show the various cases in which the optimum romance-precision-mastery sequence is either incorrectly ordered or incomplete. When I first designed these, I was surprised by the number of less than optimum patterns which exactly matched educational sequences that I had seen in practice—and indeed, some that I had designed myself.

Motivation: Plato's Socrates

Socrates and Plato worked successively to develop a particular insight into teaching. This is, that it must begin with *motivation*. Unless the student believes that he or she still has something to learn, wants to learn it, and wants to share that learning with the teacher, teaching will be ineffective. Rote memorization and operant conditioning, two methods of instruction popular at the time, are external and ineffective. They might lead to skill, but if so without insight or improvement in critical thinking or sound evaluation.

Socrates depended for his effectiveness on first-hand encounter, and did not write anything. After his execution, Plato faced the responsibility of carrying on his teacher's mission. To do this for a wide audience in space and through time, individual conversation seemed fragile. And in any case teachers with the conversational magic of Socrates seemed unlikely to appear again for a long time. Plato therefore devised a literary form, the Socratic dialogue, which he hoped could combine the permanence and publicity of writing and the challenge of Socratic conversation. His dialogues focus on the need for philosophy, and show Socrates in action with a wide range of respondents of all ages and citizen classes.

The Socratic dialogue that is a classic study of motivation is the *Meno*. Here Plato puts Socrates in touch with a young, self-satisfied and sophisticated aristocrat from the north. Meno at the outset would like to hear Socrates' opinion as to whether virtue can be taught, but he has no desire to share in an investigation of the question. He thinks he knows already; in fact, he has made public speeches on the subject. In the end, however he is caught up by an urge to share the investigation. So is the reader. Plato sets out to engage us in the question at hand, and eliminates all of the facile answers that we had accepted. When the discussion ends, such is the author's artistry that we are left just where Meno is left—challenged and motivated, partly because we have not been lectured to didactically.

Recently, when I was answering questions after a lecture on ancient Greek philosophy to a group of high school students, it occurred to me that an excellent piece of reading for secondary school philosophers would be Plato's *Meno*, provided the dialogue were rescued from scholars and given what I take to be its intended moral and interpretation. The moral in fact is multiple. In the first place, the argument shows that values (or virtues) cannot be taught either by instruction or example. (In fact, it maintains, correctly, that nothing can be taught unless the student wants to learn it.) But in the second place, the dialogue shows that virtue can be taught by the shared inquiry of the Socratic method, if that sharing is real. For, as I will show, Meno becomes better through his talk with Socrates. The fact that (as Plato's readers may know from history) Meno goes on to cowardice, treachery, and his own execution is not the result of an incorrigibly wicked nature, but the result of a bad education.

In connection with this second moral, it is worth pointing out that today we tend to reject theories of hereditary vice—though there are some defenders of the view that ignorance is hereditary—and find ourselves left with the awkward question of how we can account for the difference between good people and bad. With this in mind, I turn to the notion of the Socratic dialogue as a model for introductory philosophy, a model which combines discipline with engagement through its interaction of argument with dramatic form. This is a prologue to a new analysis of the *Meno*.

On the face of it, this dialogue offers a surprising proof by Socrates that values cannot be taught, from which it would follow that education and human excellence are irrelevant to each other. In that case, it would be a fraud for schools to claim support on the ground that they are making their students better.[1] But I do not think this surface argument is the real, or at least not the final, point of the dialogue; and I offer a more constructive and optimistic reading.

In general, scholars dealing with Socratic dialogues show a remarkable talent for saying one thing and doing another. Everyone says that

Plato intends to bring together in a new unity a dramatic form and a pattern of philosophical investigation. But having said that, almost everyone sets aside the "literary ornament" in order to concentrate on something called the "philosophical argument." This amounts to imposing a radically non-Platonic conception of philosophy on Plato, and of misreading even the argument dimension, since the action offers relevant premises as well. There are exceptions to this schizoid approach, but not enough.

Aristotle, in his *Poetics*, gives a brief account of the experiments of tragic poets looking for the "proper form" of tragedy, until it finally was stabilized with Sophocles. The same sort of history of a search for the right literary form can be written for Greek philosophy. The philosophers before Plato were experimenting with forms of communication which would be suitable to express new ideas. The list of forms they tried runs from diagram through epigram, epic and lyric, dry almanac and live conversation. The experimenters include Heraclitus, with a cryptic Oracular style; Parmenides, with a logical proof set in the frame of a philosophic journey; Empedocles, with his cosmological poetry and sharp detailed imagery; Hippias the Sophist, claiming the reference work as his invention; finally, Socrates, with engaged shared inquiry as his chosen tool. It would require a great deal of time and aesthetic sensitivity to do justice to the directions and limits which each of these forms set for the development of philosophical ideas. For the present, I can jump to the end of the story, to the stabilization of the literary form of philosophy into two families. Platonic and Aristotelian.

The Platonic form of philosophic writing derives from the tradition of Greek drama and epic, conversation and debate. It is, in its initial form, an attempt to bring the reader into a shared inquiry by including him in a Socratic conversation which is carefully left incomplete. In the background here is the Socratic idea of philosophy as engaged adventure, with debate, search, interaction of characters, change of fortune.

The Aristotelian form of philosophic writing (and philosophic lecturing) derives rather from the tradition of science, medicine, and mathematics. Its expression is that of long, coherent treatises by an impersonal omniscient author; it aims at order, scope, and objectivity. The idiosyncracies of the character of the lecturer, the behavior of his particular audiences, the excitement of risk in shared inquiry, are not relevant in this form, and are eliminated so far as possible.[2]

The second form can be conveniently labeled the "treatise" as distinguished from the "dialogue." Now, the treatise has certain merits over the dramatic dialogue. It permits literal statements that are universal in that they hold for any audience or individual. It permits of an objective precision in testing the validity and coherence of philosophic propositions. But it does these things by assuming that it is humanly possible and philosophically desirable to ascend to those heights of pure mind, disengaged from the eccentricities, individualities, and adventures of the concrete world we live in. A sign of this may be that the *ad hominem* form of argument is a fallacy to the typical Aristotelian, while for the Platonist it is one of his most effective dialectical tools.

I must confess that I am a Platonist, and see no virtue in pretending that philosophic arguments can exist in a vacuum. Not even mathematics can quite do that, as Whitehead, one of the great modern mathematicians, indicated when he ended his lecture, "Immortality," by saying of mathematics: "The exactness is a fake." I will, if I must choose, take relevance and vividness at the price of thin exactness. Since my sympathies lie with the dialogue as proper philosophic form, and since it is a form often misunderstood, I offer two case studies to show the interaction of drama and discussion that typify this form. First I look at one early Socratic dialogue, the *Lysis*; then at the *Meno*.

The cast of *Lysis* consists of Socrates, two young boys (about eleven years old), and two older boys (about eighteen). The theme is friendship; What are friends?, How are friends made? Two parts of the author's purpose are easily seen: Plato is defending Socrates against the charge of being a bad influence on the young; and he is trying to carry on the Socratic mission of inquiry. Of the four boys in the cast, each pair of the same age contrasts in temperament between one who is aggressive (Ctesippus, Menexenus) and one who is gentle (Hippothales, Lysis). Hippothales would very much like to be loved by Lysis, but Lysis dislikes him. Socrates, demonstrating the way to talk to people in order to make them friendly, directs the talk to this very topic: the cause and definition of friendship. Several commonsense notions are tried out, such as the Sophist idea that friendship is only a kind of utilitarian pursuit of advantage. Readers of Dale Carnegie's directions for winning friends and influencing people will recognize this idea in a modern incarnation. But the young men are not satisfied with this notion. Socrates suggests that perhaps love and hate are cosmic forces, and that we like and dislike other persons by a kind of law of nature. That notion had already been suggested by some cosmologists: it is tempting, because if it were true, we might build a science of love. Recent popular technology experimenting with blind dating arranged by computer is a vague echo of this idea. And if our likes and dislikes are lawlike we can see the explanation of behavior leading off to social science more generally. This view is—rather too quickly—set aside; and it is not clear how far the rejection is a result of idealism, how far of existentialism. But the whole group of characters have by now become such close friends that the boys' tutors have to break up the party by force.

Clearly, Socrates has been a good educational influence here. Equally clearly, he has left his readers with a puzzle: as far as the argument goes, there is no way we can win friends, since we do not even know what it is we are trying to win. Yet, as far as the development of the drama goes, we see Socrates using shared inquiry as a technique for making participants friends. Very well, but the reader with a logical mind remains annoyed that the scientific and cosmological accounts of friendship as natural affinity are not explored. (They are transmuted into ethical affinities instead.) But such a reader should notice that the cast consists of characters who are like and unlike with respect to age, temperament, and wisdom; that in the beginning, the pattern of their attitudes rules out the possibility of any simple "like to like" or "opposites attract" natural law governing friendship; yet that, in the end, old and young, quiet and aggressive have all become friends through the catalytic effect of Socrates.

We see the relevance of cast and character to argument even more clearly in the *Meno*. Meno, rushing up to Socrates, opens the conversation with his demand: "Let me have the word, Socrates. Can virtue be taught by precept, or by example, or is it a natural gift?" Socrates does not know but is willing to inquire. We learn immediately after his opening question that Meno was a student of the Sophist, Gorgias, a master of teaching by precept; if indeed "Sophistication" can make men better, Meno should be an ideal example. Later in the dialogue, we encounter Anytus, the Athenian statesman who later engineered the execution of Socrates; he appears as spokesman for the view that virtue is taught by example.

After Socrates refuses to offer a didactic answer to Meno's question, it takes constant persuasion on his part to get Meno to go on with the investigation. Meno, presently, exclaims that he thinks Socrates is the worst teacher he has ever seen! When Socrates leads a slave boy into seeing a geometrical proof by way of asking him questions, Meno readily agrees that Socrates has taught the boy nothing. But even if Socrates had been a teacher of geometry, this would not help decide the case for the teachability of virtue. When Socrates, Meno and Anytus cannot find any teachers of virtue, they conclude, reluctantly, that virtue cannot be knowledge; since if it were, it could be taught. And if anyone *could* teach it, he or she, being virtuous, *would* teach it. Meno becomes a better and better respondent, more interested in the argument throughout the second part of the dialogue; but he ends up puzzled by its negative conclusion. So does the reader; particularly the reader who has picked up Plato's plot, since Meno himself becomes more virtuous as the dialogue goes on. There is, then, at least one person who *can* teach virtue, Socrates. His teaching, however, is neither by didactic precept nor by example, but by shared inquiry. Since this falls outside the disjunctive notions Meno holds about possible kinds of teaching, it remains true for his sense of the term that virtue cannot be "taught." But the correct reading of the dialogue results in a much more constructive, optimistic, and better defense of Socrates than commentators have usually proposed. This result depends on taking argument and action together, and noticing how Meno changes. Even the best commentators—Klein, Sternfeld and Zyskind, Bluck—miss the full impact of this dramatic development.[3] Unfortunately for us all, one encounter with Socrates' teaching is not enough by itself to effect a permanent improvement in character; and Meno, for all his talent and his Socratic dialogue, leaves Athens continuing a star-crossed career. (One reason why Plato may have chosen him is that this career is described so bitterly by Xenophon in the *Anabasis*. If indeed vice were a matter of nature, so that some men were incorrigible, Meno would have been Xenophon's prize candidate as an example!)[4]

The *Lysis* belongs to the earliest group of Plato's writings. The *Meno* falls in the second set of Socratic dialogues in which alternatives are marked out and explored at greater length. The dialogues of this second group, though still inconclusive are more nearly complete: they end just after, rather than just before, what would be the middle of an Aristotelian structured drama. Myth and mathematics play important auxiliary roles; probably because by this time Plato had been to Italy and Sicily. His intention also seems to change: now we are shown that Socrates was not just another Sophist as Aristophanes and the Athenian public had thought. In a confrontation of life-styles, each with its spokesman, Plato plots collisions of Socrates and the teachers of success: Gorgias (and later the latter's student, Meno); Protagoras; Prodicus; Hippias; the "strong man" Callicles. There is also a confrontation of models of knowledge: Socrates defends insight into form against a storage and retrieval of information idea. Plato's world of forms includes objective value forms which is in exact opposition to the Sophistic reduction of values to arbitrary artifacts established by convention. Yet, as we have seen, the questions raised in these Socratic dialogues still go unanswered, however clearly the drama itself offers a commentary and suggests a resolution.

I would like to analyze the changes in Meno's character in more detail. The idea that there is a development of character other than a simple realization of ignorance has not been generally accepted. Even where it is tangentially recognized, it is not accompanied by the further insight that such a development exactly reverses the ostensibly pessimistic conclusion of the dialogue. So I will trace the asides and attitudes that Plato introduces to underscore the changes in character as his plot proceeds.

Meno's initial attitude is impetuousness (70A), and unwillingness to share an inquiry (at 75B he tells Socrates to answer his question for himself). Meno is also criticized for his laziness and lack of temperance (75C; compare 76A, where Meno is shameless, lazy and tyrannical, though beautiful). When, by 78D, Meno manages to define virtue in terms of wealth (erring in wisdom, temperance, and justice all at once), Socrates addresses him as "hereditary friend of the Great King." The reader who knows his Xenophon will surely appreciate that reminder. At 80A, Meno finally explodes; Socrates is like an electric eel, and the worst teacher Meno has met. In the same irascible and unreasonable mood, Meno comes up at 80D with his trick argument to trap Socrates and end their discussion. ("How can we inquire into something neither of us knows about?"). The Myth of reminiscence and the experiment with the Slave Boy mark the beginning of a change. For at 81E-82A, Meno sets a verbal trap when he asks Socrates: "Teach me that teaching is impossible." But challenged, he says: "I didn't mean to set a trap; if in any way you can explain, please do." (This reminds me that at 82E and 85D Meno agrees that Socrates is not teaching, which is crucial to my analysis of the logic of the dialogue though it is not important in tracing the character development.) At 86B, both in matters of immortality and the value of inquiry, Meno is at last persuaded; "Somehow, I like what you are saying." At 86C, we find that he has not changed entirely; he insists (intemperately, as Socrates points out) on going back to *his* question (can virtue be taught) rather than Socrates' prior question of what virtue is. This lapse does not show that Meno is indocile, incorrigible, or unimproved; the context still establishes the contrary. The hypothetical dialectic of 87A-90B finds Meno a perfect respondent: polite, intelligent, eager to follow out the reasoning. And after the interlude with Anytus—Meno is a friend of his family—at 99E Meno sides with Socrates against Anytus. At 100B, we have Meno's final speech: "That is finely put, Socrates." This is almost word-for-word the final remark of the talented Young Socrates after he has followed the technical dialectic of the Eleatic Stranger in Plato's *Statesman*.

If wisdom comes in part from removing conceit and false opinion; if courage reveals itself in the willingness to share the rigors of inquiry; and if justice is shown in the sharing of chances to ask, criticize, bring in examples; then Meno improves greatly in all three. The improvement is, as we know from hindsight, temporary; but nevertheless it is there, woven firmly into the texture of the dialogue. It has to be there, for without it two crucial points would be lost. The first is the way in which Socrates, unlike either Gorgias or Anytus, leads young men to virtue even though he does not teach it. The second point is that the temporary change is needed to prove that Plato sees Meno's star-crossed career as a genuine tragedy, not merely the consequence of an inborn vicious nature (which seems to be Xenophon's interpretation; and compare Klein's notion of Meno as an archetype of incorrigible *amathia*.)

Now, finally, we return to contemporary educational theory. And I hope it is with the realization that Plato grasped something of infinite importance to educational theory. This is that neither precept nor example will really teach anything to a student who regards the whole show as a spectator sport, though the one tactic may inform and the other may condition him. I know of no later educational theorist who does not concede the point, but I know of very few who do not forget it as soon as they have made the concession. (B. F. Skinner, for example, just assumes that his human learners are motivated though he cannot guarantee this by water deprivation as he would if they were scholar pigeons.) Is Socrates just kidding when he says he can't teach? Doesn't he teach the Slave Boy? Does anything in this story show why Anytus thought Socrates was a bad influence on young Athenians? How much did Meno learn from his past association with the famous Gorgias? What do you think about the claim that virtue cannot be taught, even though perhaps geometry can?

This last question suggests that an entire second round of discussion could center on the modern equivalent of the *Meno* thesis: that values cannot be taught. If they could be, surely there would be eager teachers of them; but can we find any institution or person with the ability to make people better, and better able to evaluate things, in the way we can find teachers of geometry or automobile repair? How far, in fact, do admonition, punishment, memorization, or admirable example work as moral educational techniques? Here we might ask a question that Socrates raises but does not follow far: is there some mistake in the model or thought picture that many of us have when we talk about teaching values? If, for example, we think of values as jewels in a case; or conditioned responses; or commands given by authorities; then should we not give up the attempt to teach them, and concentrate on learning facts and skills? (Probably what Gorgias would have recommended to a school board).

Using the *Meno* makes it easier to retain distance, generality, and objectivity in this discussion than it would be if we began with a modern example. A third moment would, ideally, be introduced by the student's discovery that Meno actually does learn something. He becomes more polite; wiser (insofar as he is now aware of his own ignorance and modest about it); more temperate; more willing to go ahead with the argument; willing to side with Socrates against Anytus; and so on. So perhaps the conclusion that seemed to follow from the argument is not the whole story. For example, how does that conclusion change if we add the premise "There exists at least one teacher of virtue" to the argument? What implications does this have for our study of philosophy?

When Whitehead argued that learning must begin with a stage of romance, he was agreeing with Plato that education is pointless without initial motivation. There is some truth in Klein's insistence that Meno is a perfect example of a stubborn non-learner. His self-satisfied conviction that he is already handsome, brave, and well-educated is a difficult state to change. In the first half of the dialogue, we see Plato applying the shock tactics of Socratic method until finally even this smug young aristocrat is provoked into wanting to learn.

The assumption shared by Plato and Whitehead is that there are two types of learning. One we can call "external"—rote memorization, accurate touch typing, repeated rules of conduct, all can be learned without any real engagement on the part of the learner. The motivation for learning of this type is almost uniformly extrinsic—as with Skinner's pigeons, it requires incremental rewards for increments of "right" behavior. The other kind of learning is internally motivated. It is the investigation of something that we want to know. So long as we feel progress is being made, the motivation to continue is internal—the learning is connected with a desire for self-realization. If the inquiry is successfully completed, we reach a stage of satisfaction. At this point, we see the field which at first attracted us as challenging, though vague, articulated into precise parts ordered in a total organizing frame. For example, Beowulf is now read as a unified powerful work, with the aid and appreciation of the technical structures of Anglo-Saxon phonetics, vocabulary, and alliteration. Euclid's geometry is the crystalline procession of the many from the one—multiple proven theorems from the abstract economy of the small initial set of axioms, postulates, and definitions. Plato's shared inquiry, in his middle dialogues, tends to end in this same way. But in order to have discipline take on meaning, and final generalization produce satisfaction with an awareness of mastery, it is essential that something like Socratic method begin the teacher's work by establishing motivation.

Precision: St. Thomas' Angel

Often we fail to appreciate the contemporary relevance of medieval discussions because they pose their questions and solutions in an entirely non-modern form. Sometimes we can get unexpected insights from reconsidering these discussions; and we may find ourselves adding new notions to the earlier treatment. A case in point is the third of St. Thomas' questions concerning teaching: "Whether a man can be taught by an angel?"[5] Once we discover what the postulated natures and powers of angels are, it becomes clear that this is a discussion with close contemporary counterparts, hence contemporary interest.

Suppose, for example, that there are beings on other planets, in systems other than our own, beings much more intelligent than we are.[6] Suppose, further, that we or they have mastered space travel enough to have an actual encounter. Can they teach us any of their superior insights? If so, what and how? Suppose they do not have senses like ours or that they have a way of knowing that does not arise by generalization from sensation and imagination? These are a first set of modern questions relating to St. Thomas'.

A second contemporary question related to this has to do with the notion of intelligence amplification. If this notion involves hidden impossibilities or contradictions (as some critics suggest it may) we may be wasting a good deal of power and hardware.[7] But if, for the specific case of angelic teaching, the concept is not contradictory, we can at least suppose the project is logically possible. Whether it proves biologically or technologically so is another matter: this will depend in part on how closely our human attitudes and skills can approach the conditions we assume for angelic teaching.

A third contemporary topic that is suggested by St. Thomas' discussion is the design of new symbolism for direct presentation of ideas—new algorithms, non-verbal symbols, etc. St. Thomas has definite ideas about how an angel would teach. He assumes that it would have a sort of telepathic access to the organs that cause images to arise in the imagination. (Dr. Wilder Penfield has caused phantasms to occur by stimulating parts of his patients' brains with electrodes.)[8] St. Thomas does not choose to discuss the further question of what an angel would do if it lacked this direct access.[9] Even a human teacher can teach externally and indirectly, he says. But he concedes that an angel can be superior in this manner of teaching as well, in his response to Objection 17.[10] Yet as a matter of pedagogical theory, the effect on the learner's imagination clearly does not absolutely require the assumed telepathic causation. One might suppose that either more refined electrical stimulation of the Penfield type, or physical action on the relevant brain areas through the senses, would be able to produce the same symbols and similitudes as those caused by the postulated angelic action. This is a point where the contemporary reader needs to extend and supplement St. Thomas' discussion, and a point where its relevance is quite clear.

With these contemporary analogues in mind, let us turn to a more detailed analysis of the disputed question itself. Rather than taking up the seventeen Objections and Replies separately, I present a summary statement of the result.

Angels are intermediate in knowledge and power between man and God. If they can teach us, it must be by a third kind of teaching, intermediate between divine and human.[11] God teaches directly and internally by an inner illumination and grace, acting directly on both intellect and will.[12] Men teach externally and discursively, by conventional signs.[13] (In the fourth Objection and Reply to Question 2 of the present set, St. Thomas argues that a use of words is the optimum manner of human teaching. While this is in accord with the Aristotelian tradition, namely, teaching by treatises based on lectures, further reflection is in order before the first prize is given to the discursive, lecture method.)[14] We learn by insight. Learning begins with phantasms in the imagination which result from the action of sensation. Eventually, we recognize the images and separate out the formal properties from the individuating qualities associated with them in imagination.[15] Though angels are not omniscient (they do not know future contingencies)[16] they are superior to us in their way of knowing. Angels know forms, essences, and principles by direct insight and thus they do not depend on sensation to provide the material basis for that knowledge. Nevertheless, angels can also be aware of the complex immaterial mental phantasms that figure in human cognition. (These, since they are mental and incorporeal, can be cognized without needing physical objects acting on senses as their causes. But it seems, as St. Thomas' analysis proceeds, that an angel's knowledge of phantasms is derivative from a prior knowledge of species and essences. For human knowledge, on the other hand, the physical sensations and resulting mental images must be prior in the process of knowing.)[17] Not everyone would agree to the premise that angels have this kind of access to human minds. Emanuel Swedenborg, for example, had a different view: he held that angels cannot be aware of any properties deriving from physical or psychological space and time.[18]

Angels cannot act as God does: internally, immediately, invincibly.[19] Nor can they act directly to determine a human will: for our wills, we are responsible.[20] But St. Thomas argues that while an angel cannot coerce the human will, it can command intellectual attention by emphatic presentation, resulting in "wonder," a description fitting solidly in the Aristotelian tradition. (But, if so, we can see that the development of the notion of wonder as a precondition for learning is on a head-on collision course with Descartes' notion. Descartes undertook to prove that men wonder too much!).

As to the details of angelic teaching, the parties to the discussion with St. Thomas agree (as part of the Resolution, which escapes the 17 Objections) that angels can act directly on matter (on the ground that "a higher order of causality can modify a lower.")[21] As a particular case of such causal action, an angel can, as we have noted, act on the material organs responsible for human imagination, leading to the direct production of phantasms in the human mind. This way of teaching is a third way, intermediate between the *interior* teaching of God and the *exterior* teaching of men.[22]

Angelic teaching seems to differ from teaching that is merely human in three ways. First, it differs in *scope*: angels know more facts, and principles, and causes than we do, and so can extend human knowledge by instruction in these.[23] Second, in *clarity*, if, as St. Thomas argues, an angelic mind can become continuous with and strengthen our own.[24] (For theological reasons, three interpretations of such angelic illumination cannot be accepted. First, as noted above, the illumination cannot be regarded as coercing the human will.[25] Second, it must be recognized that there is no necessity for angelic mediation between God and our own inner natural light.[26] Third, the common characteristic of ilumination must not be interpreted as implying a single active mind for all mankind, or for all angels and mankind.[27]) Third, the two kinds of teaching differ in their *kinds of order*. An angel, with a direct grasp of essences, can devise similitudes and phantasms which will not confuse or obscure the essential species they symbolize—or, more exactly, will confuse and obscure them as little as possible, some confusion being inevitable since we are dealing with individuated images in a student's imagination.[28] Insight on the student's part will come easily because of the super-cognizability of his imagination's display. In the first of the ways in which angel and human differ, the angel is like a much more knowledgeable human teacher. In the second, the angel is like a much less powerful Divine Illuminator. In the third, the angelic teacher works in an intermediate way which seems to be its own.

Joining in this discussion with my own comments and objections, I ask first of all whether St. Thomas does not rate human teachers too low? It is probably true that if we take the didactic lecture method as main paradigm, human teaching is external and discursive, and the symbolism it employs is very indirect.[29] (This paradigm is accepted by St. Thomas on the basis of Aristotle's work.[30] But if Aristotle's own lecture notes had been transmitted illustrated with the various diagrams and other visual aids he referred to, his admirers might recognize that various kinds of symbolism can be parts or moments of a good discursive method.)[31] But consider a human teacher who shares St. Thomas' insight that there can be a third way of teaching. Although it is true that an angel using this way avoids any distortions of sense perception by acting directly on the organs of the productive imagination, this may not be very different from optimum action through the senses on the organs in question. In considering this, let us experiment for ourselves to see how far we can approach this third way.[32]

What would St. Thomas' angel think about the use of a cheap calculator to give patterns to our system of number? Does this new aid help us connect the pure concepts of set theory with the more particular phantasms which fall under them? Or might the angel reject this aid, fearing that the human student would take the pictures and buttons as literally equivalent to mathematics, and so never move beyond imagination to abstraction? (If the number seven means only a design shaped like this, "7", there would certainly be a loss of insight in the supposed interests of practical facility.) But we might tell the angel at this point that the multiplication table never did guarantee any easy transition from the memorized symbolic substitutions to any further abstract illumination. I can only suggest here that a sympathetic angel would see no great merit in our traditional rote work on computation, school grade after school grade. It did not even, for many of us, build desirable traits of character. And a machine does this sort of thing more quickly, tirelessly, and better. But the angelic teacher must now look for symbolic ways to show us what the logical and formal relations are that the calculator combines and quantifies. The gained time, released from years of computational routine, may be used for some more concrete activity—soccer, musical composition, or watching television. (Another new medium whose educational value I would inquire of the angel.)

One demonstration of new, clear, sensible symbolism as an aid to human learning and thought is given by A. N. Whitehead in his *Introduction to Mathematics*. His account seems to recognize moments in intellectual history when human genius achieves a level close to that which St. Thomas reserves for angelic teaching.

> By relieving the brain of all unnecessary work, a good notation sets it free to concentrate on more advanced problems, and in effect increases the mental power of the race. Before the introduction of the Arabic notation, multiplication was difficult, and the division even of integers called into play the highest mathematical faculties. . . .
>
> So in mathematics, granted that we are giving any serious attention to mathematical ideas, the symbolism is an immense simplification . . . it represents an analysis of the ideas of the subject in an almost pictorial representation of their relations to each other . . . It is interesting to note how important for the development of science a modest-looking symbol may be. It may stand for the *emphatic* [my italics[33]] presentation of an idea, often a very subtle idea, and by its existence make it easy to exhibit the relation of this idea to all the complex trains of ideas in which it occurs. For example, take the most modest of all symbols, namely, 0, which stands for the *number* zero . . . It is in a way the most civilized of all the cardinals, and its use is only forced on us by the needs of cultivated thought. Many important services are rendered by the symbol 0, which stands for the number zero.[34]

I think this view is correct; and I believe the result of such successful new design is like that of angelic teaching. (Note the comments in the passage that it "increases the mental power of the race" and that "a modest-looking symbol" may stand for "the emphatic presentation of an idea, often a very subtle idea.") In that case, we may want to apply St. Thomas' discussion to the three contemporary topics I cited in the beginning of this section, without also introducing axioms that would ascribe telepathic power and non-material causality to any superior intelligences we may create or encounter. (Or we may not want to do without these assumptions; there is considerable contemporary interest in parapsychology both here and in the Soviet Union.) We may still want to agree that high intelligence is contagious when we encounter it directly (which we notice in exchanges with high human intelligence). This could be described as a strengthening of our own intellectual light by the presence and continuity of an intelligence brighter than our own.[35] We may want to continue discussing the question—for example, by proving that Whitehead's enthusiasm for symbolism does not show that human inventiveness ever attains the level of St. Thomas' third way of teaching.[36] My own aim is the more modest one of showing how a technical medieval discussion can teach something about teaching technique to a modern reader.

Presence: An Adventure of a Yale Lecturer

One dimension of my discussion of teaching is still lacking: the fact is that the presence and attitude of a teacher is a crucial aspect of learning and of teaching. The reason for this lies, at least in part, in the complex nature of time.

Several years ago, when I was lecturing to two hundred students in a course on the history of ancient philosophy, an arresting advertisement came in my mail. An educational film company had just put together a series on the history of philosophy by expert lecturers. For a modest rental fee I could replace my own inexpert efforts with polished professional performances. Not only that, but in the interests of dialogue each film ended with a brief filmed question and answer

114

period. I was convinced, somehow, that my transformation from lecturer to overpaid projectionist would not be an educationally desirable thing. But I decided to take the question to my captive lecture audience. They all preferred me to the film, and told me why. "You are right here when you are lecturing, and it isn't already decided what's going to happen. You might back off of the platform, or lose a page of notes, or even think of some spontaneous witty analogy. The film is edited, *and it is over.*"

The truth that those remarks reflect is that communication in a shared present is radically different from fixed messages beamed into the present from a completed past. Periodic eccentricities and failures are one symptom of this difference. The lecturer concludes: "And thus, so far as the availability of Aristotle's Prime Mover for religious purposes is concerned—is concerned—dammit these notes are illegible. But He isn't." No film or written text records the kind of jeopardy that present creative communication faces. And if periodic failures occur, so more frequently do successes.

The basis for this effect is the radical difference between the three aspects of time. But more precise analyses are controversial. Some phenomenologists treat teaching as a form of telepathy. (This is a possibility that Whitehead leaves open, pending empirical determination.) St. Thomas, as we have noted, treats this as a case of strengthened intellectual illumination. Plato's Socrates, in his method of inquiry, underscores the uncertainty and risk of investigation. (The Socratic dialogue is a unique exception to my remark above that no finished written text captures the quality of present communication.) In his earlier writing, Whitehead talks about the observer in nature and the other things and persons that share his or her time system, and introduces the term "cogredience." This is a concrete set of observations from which frames of reference for coordinate systems are built by extensive abstraction.

I do not know how to adjudicate these alternative suggestions. All I do contend is that there is a difference between shared *present* being with someone and *past* archives or *future* fantasies. This difference is recognized in almost any concrete discussion of education, though it tends to get lost in discussions of the more arcane and abstract reaches of educational theory and technology. Thus, while a superhuman teacher could use technology and new notation to replace routine student drudgery, there is no question that the plan will fail if the living teacher tries to abscond, leaving us with rooms full of handsome hardware.[37]

CHAPTER NINE
Knowing: Whitehead's Third Stage

The outcome of successful teaching is the student's seeing as an interesting single whole the qualitative and structural details he or she has examined one by one. Effective planning for such a final stage of generalization and satisfaction includes correct sequence. In an earlier discussion, we pointed out that there is one most favorable pattern for learning which matches the phases of existence of very small entities and the careers of civilizations alike. For the maximum effectiveness of curricular design, we said, these basic phases of concrete development must be acknowledged. To see the implications of this suggestion, and also to test it, note that adventures in learning are far more complex than the either/or phases of the simplest physical entities. Being more complex, they are subject to various types and degrees of frustration and distortion. These will not preclude learning, but will needlessly lessen its effect.

Taking the optimum pattern as consisting of the three stages of romance (R), precision (P), and satisfaction (S), in that order, we can construct one table of incomplete, and one of disordered, deviations. These could all be described as ways to miss the mark for any given educational program. In the first place, consider planning patterns that involve omission of stages (primes indicate absent phases; thus R' means there is no R stage).

$$(O1) \quad R'P'S'$$
$$(O2) \quad R'P'S$$
$$(O3) \quad R'P \; S$$

$$(O4) \quad R \ P'S'$$
$$(O5) \quad R \ P'S$$
$$(O6) \quad R \ P \ S$$

Pattern (O1) is clearly anaesthesia, or pure detention. (O2) would limit education to uninteresting and unspecified generalization. It may be, as we suggested above, than an angel could actually learn in this way, seeing the concrete as a fall from the abstract. But if so, it is still clear that this is not the way an angel would teach *us*. (O3) is a tempting simplification of planning. It means to get to work with no preliminary nonsense, and so to have maximum efficiency. Unfortunately, it has no motivation and no interest. As a result, in any actual case there would be no directed transition from P to S. Teaching by rote in the hope that this will end up developing appreciation and insight has been often tried, but not successfully. (O4) is stimulating for a while, but wholly undirected. The unstructured excitement loses its charm when it becomes evident that no structure is emerging. Then all sense of progress, of temporal direction is lost. (O5) is often tried in introductory or survey courses. It is discussed below as a variation of the S-P-R design. (O6) is the optimum, because the most realistic plan, which makes it the most natural and efficient as well.

In planning for learning, it is clear that stages can be transposed as well as omitted. Many educational plans, correct in recognizing the need for all three stages, actually adopt transposed orders of them. The transposed sequences are:

$$(T1) \quad S \ P \ R$$
$$(T2) \quad S \ R \ P$$
$$(T3) \quad P \ S \ R$$
$$(T4) \quad P \ R \ S$$
$$(T5) \quad R \ S \ P$$
$$(T6) \quad R \ P \ S$$

(T1) and (T2) are rationalist models. They are eminently attractive to the scholar who has already mastered and ordered his field, now enjoying a retrospective survey of it. And this metaphor of the surveyor—looking from a height rather than running through a swamp—is taken over by the survey course. The trouble is, the articulating concepts are presented to the beginning learner with no indication of their content. But abstract axiom systems, such as Cantor's set theory, are on first encounter uninteresting and empty. If the course designer tries to correct for the apparent uninterestingness, his plan becomes S R P, and will fail from want of any adequate S P connection; R here does not serve as a middle term. (Here I am turning my back on many teachers in the Platonic tradition. That tradition is constantly tempted by the thought that since knowledge is concerned with form, independent of any one given specific example, we can teach pure forms without any content.) (T3) and (T4) are objectionable on almost every ground, I think. A sign that they are not very good is the constant need to supplement them with external motivation. Another sign is that the items learned in the P mode, without structural comprehension, are forgotten almost as rapidly as they are learned. (Many of us who learned languages for specific purposes in this way in the army forgot them totally almost on the day we went back to civilian life.) (T5), again, will fail to offer motivation for the P stage; and while we may be excited at the breadth of the view, its details remain an unarticulated blur. This is an introductory course or text of the "Romance of x" style. The R S transition is not natural: the student fascinated by the Michelson-Morley experiment is not ready for a sudden collision with Maxwell's equations. These may still look exciting, but it is the excitement of cabalistic symbols. (T6) is untransposed, what we advocate as the best construction of learning sequences.

As an addendum to this, let me add a further note on the need to include the S phase, that of satisfaction, and consequently avoid sequences (O1) and (O4). It seems to me that our teachers have the attitude that high-school learning is relatively unimportant. So the student, rather than feeling pleased at having mastered the periodic table, is given the notion that maybe he will come to the real truth in college. (But in that case, why has he gone through this exercise in high school?) The college student, in turn, is not encouraged to be complacent; it will only be in graduate school that truths worth knowing will be encountered. Nor do we even allow the graduate student a sense of real achievement. This constant detraction from what is being accomplished now, at each stage, is a sure prescription for frustration.

I once compared an educational system with no moments of satisfaction to a monotonous super-highway. It is a road with no points of interest and with changes of velocity only at the toll-booths set along the way. The student turns off, not because he has come to any selected destination, but just because he can no longer afford to pay the toll. Whitehead, in his earliest work on the teaching of mathematics, had already seen the need for this moment. Even on the small scale of single assigned problems, he wanted the student working out the exercise not only to do it, and do it right, but also to realize that he had done it! Whitehead expresses the same idea in a more generalized form in "The Rhythm of Education" and in *Process and Reality*, his major philosophical work, wherein the stage of satisfaction is the last phase of concrescence or actualization of every actual entity.

CHAPTER TEN
Importance and Cosmology

As we have seen, so long as science was taken for metaphysics, that is, as the sole method and description of reality, a good deal of human experience had to be set aside as illusory and unimportant. During the period when logical positivism was dominant in academic philosophy, the more speculative schemes of thought found theology and divinity schools a congenial home. Perhaps it is partly for this historic reason that process philosphy has had so much of its impact in religion and theology.

The first problem with science posing as metaphysics, was that its austere abstractions offered no justification for our intrusive human conviction of our importance. In a world machine, what we do is predetermined, and what is done to us is irrelevant. But we do have strong intuitive convictions, suppressed only by years of conditioning, that we are sensitive, free, creative, and somehow part of a cosmos where value and purpose have a place. In such a world, our feeling of importance is justified because we *are* important and at home.

The vision we are describing may be called a "religious vision," and may be recognized as a common human experience underlying various religions. But this vision, like vague ideals and general Platonic forms, is largely unspecified and incomplete. To give it definiteness and force, religions have identified this general cosmic awareness with specific sacred objects, rituals, claimed miracles and revelations, in physical time and space. This gives an added concreteness to what we feel, but at a high price. Once symbols, myths, and metaphors have been transformed into dogmas and historic facts, all religion finds itself in conflict with science, and each religion with every other. The conflict

121

with science occurs because it is, and should be, science that uses its methods to test the truth of statements regarding matters of fact. Myth, miracle, and metaphor, *if we transmute them to factual claims*, fail these tests. Fossils show evidence of evolution; measurements of whales' throats show that they can't swallow people; the center of the earth is molten rock, not a concentric-circled Hell. Nor do claimed historical miracles survive the work of the critical historian any better than the myth of hell survives the work of the geologist.

Transferring the general cosmic vision to specific doctrinal terms also creates relations of contradiction and exclusion between specific religions. If the issues between religions each claiming an exclusive truth are indeed questions of fact, only one of them can be true. One might want to reject scientific testing as a criterion of truth and appeal instead of to revelation. But even so, between two different revelations each making claims to exclusive insight, the relation of contradiction holds.

It is not my intention to end my discussion of education with a rejection of all religions or the endorsement of any particular one. But I do want to point out two implications for religion of process cosmology. The first is that all religions share and try to express a single cosmic vision. The vision is not factual and precise, and the several alternative expressions must be seen as symbolic, mythical, and metaphorical. By a mistaken insistence that each is literal and exclusively true, religions lose sight of their inspiration.[1]

In the second place, process philosophy holds that there can and must be mutual harmony between science, cosmology and theology. An implication of this view is that classical Western theology must be modified to harmonize with what science finds to be actual. As a result, process philosophy leads to what Charles Hartshorne and others call "non-classical theology." The sort of change involved may be illustrated by the different treatments of divine omniscience by the two views. The classical doctrine is that God knows, as simultaneous and actual, all temporal fact. The non-classical view is that, since there are as yet no future facts, though God knows all that there is to be known, there are no future facts for Him to know. A corollary of this is that God's knowledge of the world changes with time. I have introduced this illustration because it is an interesting extension of process cosmology into the areas of religion, theology, and religious education.

My present conclusion, however, does not depend either on a critique of religion or a transformation of metaphysics into theology. Process philosophy, as I would develop it, remains viable and consistent without including a supreme being. Process philosophy agrees that if there is supernatural knowledge or experience, this lies beyond its own sphere. But within the natural order, process cosmology offers a final vision of ourselves and the world which reaches beyond science and the practical, and which should be the final satisfaction that concludes our education.[2]

We are, as we feel we are, free and creative agents. Logic and physics deal with abstractions that hide this from us because they leave out of account the different modalities of time—its past, present, and future—but we as philosophers can correct for that selective attention. We are in fact, as we sometimes think we are and sometimes think we are not, sharers in larger communities. Societies, civilization, cosmic advance, are larger wholes to which we belong. We do not belong to these simply as insulated separate parts; these larger unities are actually parts of our own individual identities. Natural science had made this seem implausible by its selective attention to the insulating function of space; and this view has far too often been taken over by the social sciences, by business, and by government.

Again, in treating space, science has missed important facts by insisting on a useful but selective abstraction. By its treatment of space as insulator, it has ignored the way in which individuals and communities *are* really together. Worse, it has left out of account any suggestion of the way in which different, separate, nations, religions, or cultures, may *possibly* be together. Instead, this model—designed to deal with small, hard particles in flight and collision—represents all reality as relations of competition and exclusion. The process cosmology notion of a larger identity extends beyond human institutions: we are also in a larger environment than man made, an evolving natural world of living things of other species and scales of size. Realistic self-realization is thus not the paranoid defensive response of an isolated center of sensitivity to pain and pleasure: rather, it is a growth that has taken into account an environment as wide as the cosmos.

What the world will become, and what humanity will become in it, is being decided by each of us in our present choices. In a world in process, the quality and structure of the future are actualized by our creative selections in the present time. There is every cosmological reason, therefore, for our intuitive sense of responsibility. If the natural science model of physical causality were metaphysically complete, as well as being correct in a limited context, such a sense of responsibility would indeed be irrational. (This seems the view of Sartre, Camus, and other existentialists: that the sense of responsibility is there, insistent; but by criteria of rationality, it is absurd. Process thought may offer a new alternative analysis of rationality.)

Beyond this responsibility, each of us, as a concrete individual, is valuable. We are unique concrete beings, with creativity and style, aesthetically interesting. But social science and practical administration use selective abstract concepts and categories which deliberately rule out these qualities. Social engineering, industrial efficiency, military manpower, all are abstractions of this type. And this tendency to ignore the aesthetic quality of individual experience and life style is partly a consequence of the mistaken notion that the abstractions developed by physics—space, time, causality, determinism—are the only realistic ideas available to the social scientist. Process philosophy suggests an alternative: attention to the aesthetic qualities of other persons, of our social community, of nature, of life styles, of works of fine art. One thing this emphasis on concrete seeing aims at is to avoid—through lack of imagination—missed opportunities for pleasure, interest, and adventure.

Finally, we see that we are spatially and temporally at home in a cosmic community. We see that we are creatively sharing in, and so responsible for, cosmic temporal advance and evolving creativity. We are capable of creating and experiencing values of aesthetic intensity, unlike the quality-blind fundamental observers of physics, whom we met in an earlier chapter. And we are aware that because of the actual relations of space, time, process, fact, and value, we have importance and immortality.

CHAPTER ELEVEN

Immortality: Whitehead's Lecture and Plato's *Phaedo*

Our importance comes from the fact of our immortality. We are aware of this in a vague but powerful intuitive way. But the immortality which we discover in cosmology is not the concrete personal continuation of personality and sensation which we might naively wish for. Much as powerful but diffuse religious vision is transformed into the concrete doctrine of an individual religion, the vision of importance is often translated into a doctrine of personal persistence in a literal form that goes well beyond the limits of philosophy.

Plato, in the *Phaedo*, sets the stage for later discussions as his Socrates explores the various ways in which the soul is and is not immortal. What he would like to prove is personal immortality; but it is a myth, not a proof, that brings this final conversation to its close. On the level of cosmic process, Socrates begins, we are part of an ongoing vital flow through time. We lend our energy and our causal power to this ongoing history, and our contributions are dynamic energies and eddies forever in its flow. But our role in this process may be conceived impersonally; (and in fact this is the way that many Indian and Eastern philosophies conceive it). On the level of timeless truth, we are able to know forms outside the limitations of space and time. Socrates argues that, if like is known by like, this ability proves that as knowers we are somehow non-natural. The argument is certainly right insofar as we are identical with what we know. For the angel of St. Thomas, the identity would hold. But for ourselves as human beings, our existence is temporal as well as beyond time. This second moment of the *Phaedo* shows why we feel that we are *more* than temporal, but it does not establish that we are *nothing but* that timeless form. Neo-Platonism and other mysticisms argue their cosmological case from the vivid insight into this reach of the self beyond time. But the mystic, even Spinoza's sage, returns from meditation to existence and conversation.

The causal power that we exercise and the responsibility that goes with it is a third fact the *Phaedo* brings forward in its investigation. In response to Simmias' suggestion that the soul is related to its body epiphenomenally, as a harmony is related to the strings of a lyre, Socrates points out that the soul causes the body's behavior, rather than the other way around. I first decide to move my arm, and then the arm moves; whereas if Simmias were right, the causal action would run the opposite way. This causality gives us power, direction, and decisiveness in our cosmic roles. It is this, I think, that is expressed by Sartre as an irrational but inescapable sense of responsibility. But again, while immortality in this sense of trans-physical causal power may be granted, it is not the answer to the question of any sort of personal survival, which is the issue Socrates and his friends concentrate on.

Our choices bring value into the world. We are a bridge between timeless forms, in a domain of possibility, and the irreversible actuality which our creative actions establish in history. The quality of the cosmos, its value, is contributed to by our own value selections. It is his vision of what is good that constrains Socrates to remain in prison. In his lecture "Immortality," two millenia later, Whitehead stresses the identity of the individual with the values that each chooses to incarnate. The ideal offers an identity beyond the actual, but only when the actual embraces it. Whitehead here, like Socrates in his response to Simmias, wants it to be clear that the abstrct mechanistic hypothesis of science and the analytic niceties of logic are not relevant to the intuition that is expressed in this conclusion.

In Plato's dialogue, if we are typical of the cosmos, it may be that everything is ordered by value, by what is good. In that case, if it is good for anyone to have personal immortality, we can hope the cosmic order will award it. But this is a myth that concludes the *Phaedo*; and it is plain that it is not put forward as any literal demonstration. Socrates projects his final hope in a concrete story about a world order where geology and Orphic religion coincide, and about an ideal world where the gods—living, not sculptured in stone—greet us outside their otherworldly temples.

Whitehead, in his lecture, stresses the relevant identity of the self with the values it chooses. He does not offer a counterpart to the Myth of the True Earth in Plato's *Phaedo*. He does, however, show that process philosophy is consistent with a world order organized for realization of the good. There can be, and Whitehead is sure there is, a God within this system. He or She may not be portrayed as an Apollo or Aphrodite with whom we can shake hands; but He or She may be represented as a present companion, sharing and forever conserving our feelings and creations as we move through space and time.

While Whitehead and some of his followers develop a process theology as an extension of cosmology, our educational theory need not, at least for the present, follow them that far. But it must follow far enough to agree that the awareness of our immortality in the ways in which we have seen that we do have it, and our consequent awareness of our cosmic importance, lead toward a philosophic vision and an aesthetic satisfaction which should be the final moments of education.

Looking back, we recall that for the ultimately simple actual occasion, existence is an abrupt achievement. Its concrescence passes into objective immortality, and it remains forever through time as a datum, a fact available for the future. It may be transmitted intact, or recombined, or ignored. Even on this simplest level, Whitehead finds, in the transformation of the vital present into a closed but indestructible past, there is a kind of immortality. The notion that past deeds and events persist, haunting the present, is an intuition on a higher level of complexity of this same kind.

Something of this same sense of the persistence of the past, a past no longer active with present vigor, is expressed in Bashō's "Ruin of Takadachi Fort:"

> Summer grasses wave;
> Brave warriors' deeds
> Mist of a dream.

Mist-like, in contrast to the present grass, but still the deeds are there.

This persistence of the past is a persistence of value and achievement for such larger, more complex entities as species and civilizations. For us, the ideals of human individuals are made into concrete choices and events, and these persist as well. They lend their energy and quality to history, and remain for later appreciation and perhaps emulation. As combinations of timeless forms, values are not temporal. And just insofar as our personal identities consist in our choices of coherent sets of ideals, we share this transcendence of temporality. But spatial and timeless ideals are only outlines and potentialities for actual specific values; these require the determinateness of space and time.

The peculiar cosmic role of each human individual can be seen in the responsibility of each as creative agent. It is by an *appreciation* of value as future, *selection* of it as present, and *conservation* of it as past, that we as individuals achieve our cosmic importance. And this may be as far as cosmology can take us in a search for immortality. Whether we can add detail to it or not, this view of cosmic reality is the final stage of generalization, the final satisfaction that is the goal and the outcome of a truly realistic system of education.

Notes

Introduction

1. There are assumptions about the nature of causality and time underlying the seemingly simple formalism of Chapter 4 that need much more exploration. A start in that exploration is my "Metaphysical Systems and the Study of Time," *International Society for the Study of Time, Proceedings*, Vol. III (New York: Springer Verlag, 1978) pp. 1–21. These proceedings are hereafter cited as *Proceedings*.

Chapter One

1. David Eugene Smith and J. Ginsburg, *Numbers and Numerals* (New York: Teachers College, Columbia University, 1937) pp. 29–31, has illustrations of medieval multiplication and long division matrices.

2. René Thom, " 'Modern' Mathematics: An Educational and Philosophical Error?" *American Scientist* 59 (1971), p. 695 ff.

Chapter Three

1. For a treatment of logic with tenses, cp. Robert S. Brumbaugh, "Applied Metaphysics: Truth and Passing Time," *Review of Metaphysics*, 25 (1966), pp. 642–66.

2. Whitehead's criticism of 17th-century physics is given a particularly clear statement in *Science and the Modern World* (New York: The Macmillan Company, 1925), Chapters 3 and 13, abbreviated SMW.

3. New options are offered for twentieth-century physics by the theories of relativity and quantum theory. Whitehead offers some exploration of this in SMW, Chapters 8 and 9; the incorporation of the new ideas from physics into his philosophy of process is one central aim of *Process and Reality* (New York: The Macmillan Company, 1929; Corrected Edition, ed. by David Ray Griffin and Donald W. Sherburne, New York: The Free Press, A Division of Macmillan Publishing Co., Inc., 1978), abbreviated PR.

4. A full catalogue of inherited fallacies would include all cases where there is inappropriate acceptance of a set of abstractions, generated by selective attention, as a complete and adequate account of something concrete. The ideas of empty space, of

universal mechanical determinism, of hard and fast environmental limits to social progress, of a dualism of primary and secondary qualities, are some cases in point. See Chapter 1 above.

5. See Chapter 2 above.

6. Sir Charles P. Snow, *The Two Cultures and the Scientific Revolution* (Cambridge: Cambridge University Press, 1959).

7. The selective character of perception comes out clearly in Whitehead's *Symbolism* (New York: The Macmillan Company, 1927) and *Religion in the Making* (New York: The Macmillan Company, 1926).

8. The various kinds of abstraction that give rise to abrupt hierarchies are not explored in SMW. The set would certainly include pragmatic abstractions, as well as taxonomic and perceptual types. On this point, see R. S. Brumbaugh, "Whitehead as a Philosopher of Education: Action, Abstraction, Satisfaction," *Educational Theory* 15 (1965) pp. 277–81.

9. In PR, God is responsible for the presentation of possibilities organized in graded relevance. The organizing principles seem to be three: logical compossibility, spatio-temporal compatibility, and aesthetic compatibility. (The alternatives to this third relation are either neutralization, disintegration, or violent uncombinability.) On this point, some very suggestive ideas are presented in the discussion of non-conformal propositions by Donald Sherburne, "Reason and the Claim of Ulysses: A Comparative Study of Two Rationalists, Blanshard and Whitehead," *Idealistic Studies*, 4 (1974), pp. 18–34.

10. SMW, Chapter 5. One wonders what further metaphysical insights we could have if our aesthetic observers list included Keats and Coleridge, or Heraclitus and Empedocles? (In particular, some participants in a 1978 "Process and Praxis" Conference on Authority advanced a view of creativity very like the mighty-fountain imagery of Coleridge's "Kubla Khan".)

11. SMW, Chapter 5.

12. To study pattern and sequence, one must be able to spatialize successive configurations by abstraction from process. If the abstracted patterns are mistakenly supposed to exhaust the concrete flow, the result is the sort of false metaphysics which Bergson attacked in his *An Introduction to Metaphysics*, trans. T. E. Hulme (New York and London: G. P. Putnam's Sons, 1912).

13. Nathaniel M. Lawrence, "Whitehead: The Rhythm of Nature," in R. S. Brumbaugh and N. M. Lawrence, *Philosophers on Education*, (Boston: Houghton Mifflin, 1963) pp. 154–85; also, "Nature and the Educable Self in Whitehead," *Educational Theory*, 15 (1965), pp. 205–16.

14. George Allan, *A Whiteheadian Approach to the Philosophy of History*, Dissertation, Yale University, New Haven, 1973.

15. J. G. Whitrow, *The Natural Philosophy of Time*, (2nd edition, Oxford: Clarendon Press 1980); "Reflections on the History of the Concept of Time," *Proceedings I*, pp. 1–12.

16. A particularly clear presentation of this doctrine and the problem it poses is given by Newton P. Stallknecht, "The Theory of God as Supreme Being," in N. P. Stallknecht and R. S. Brumbaugh, *The Spirit of Western Philosophy* (New York: Longmans and Green, 1950) pp. 206–10.

17. Aristotle's Prime Mover is a central topic in *Metaphysics* Lambda. See Sir William D. Ross' discussion in *Aristotle's Metaphysics*, ed. Sir W. D. Ross, 2 vols.

(Oxford: Clarendon Press 1924), "Aristotle's Theology," I, cliii–cliv; note the final negative appraisal: " . . . the God whom he sets up is inadequate to meet the demands of the religious consciousness."

18. Cp. The Leibniz-Clarke correspondence (ed. H. G. Alexander, Manchester, 1956). Also D. Corish, "Time, Space and Free Will: The Leibniz-Clarke Correspondence," in *Proceedings III*, pp. 635–53; and my "Comments," ibid., pp. 656–58.

19. Whitehead's systematic view is given in the final section of PR. Various metaphors that religions have used to describe God—Emperor, sage, companion—are discussed in *Religion in the Making*.

Chapter Four

1. The decade of the 1970's saw a "genetic anomaly" defense of a confessed killer introduced both in an Australian and in a United States criminal court. It was allowed in part by the former but rejected by the latter.

2. Time serves to establish causal connection only in the world of the *First Critique*. Concepts and intuitions are related there by a schema; in the later two critiques, a type and symbol serve instead for mediation.

3. Henri L. Bergson, *Time and Free Will*, trans. F. Pogson (New York: The Macmillan Company, 1910).

4. Alfred North Whitehead, *The Function of Reason* (Princeton: Princeton University Press, 1929).

5. For a discussion of the difficulties of determinism as it appears in the classical version of the atomic theory, see R. S. Brumbaugh, *The Philosophers of Greece* (Albany: State University of New York Press, 1981).

6. Correspondence with Donald Sherburne first suggested to me that these values might be identified with Whitehead's own classification of propositions into conformal, non-conformal, and an implied third type, partially conformal. John Cobb discussed the implications of this for education at a Conference at Claremont in 1980. My conformal values are $= 1$ or $= 0$ for the past and for atemporal statements; $\neq 0$ is the partially conformal value of an option which can be chosen in a given present; $\neq 1$ is the noncommittal status of propositions referring forward to unspecified future possibility.

7. Note that negation is a stronger relation than simple otherness. It introduces definiteness when it operates on indefinite values (thus $\sim \neq 1) = 1, \sim (\neq 0) = 0$). Cp. Plato's *Sophist*, where motion is the negation of rest but only different from being.

8. Aristotle's sea-fight, *De Interpretatione*.

9. Aristotle rejects causal inference to future conclusions using efficient causes as middle terms. His theory of choice would, I think, include my $\neq 0$ values as future.

10. R. S. Brumbaugh, "Metaphysical Systems and the Study of Time," *Proceedings III*, pp. 1–21.

11. This reads the implication relation, $p \supset q$, as "p may be a cause of q", i.e., "not p and not $\sim q$" ($\sim (p \cdot \sim q)$). It is certain that this fails only when p is true and q is false. This reading removes most of the supposed "paradoxes of material implication." See N. P. Stallknecht and R. S. Brumbaugh, *The Spirit of Western Philosophy*, op. cit., pp. 487–88.

12. R. S. Brumbaugh, "Applied Metaphysics: Truth and Passing Time, *Review of Metaphysics*, op. cit.

13. Arthur N. Prior, *Time and Modality* (Oxford: The Clarendon Press, 1957).

14. Stephen Körner, *Abstraction in Science and Morals* (Cambridge: Cambridge University Press, 1971).

15. This is treated in detail in Chapter 5 below.

Chapter Five

1. This criticism applies particularly to the main orientation of Richard Gale's anthology, *The Philosophy of Time* (New York: Doubleday Anchor Books, 1967); and to the approach of C. F. P. Sutterheim, "Time in Language and Literature," in J. P. Fraser, ed., *The Voices of Time* (New York: George Braziller, 1966), pp. 163–80. It does not apply to the approach of Nathaniel Lawrence, e.g., in his "Levels of Language in Discourse about Time," *Proceedings* III, pp. 22–53.

2. For an alternative non-Platonic account, see R. S. Brumbaugh, "Metaphysical Presuppositions and the Study of Time," *Proceedings* III, pp. 1–21. For a criticism of this method of treatment, see G. K. Plochmann, "The Cross That Bears Philosophy," *Midwestern Journal of Philosophy*, Winter, 1975.

3. R. S. Brumbaugh, "Kinds of Time: An Excursion in Metaphysics," in I. C. Lieb, ed., *Experience, Existence, and the Good* (Carbondale: Southern Illinois University Press, 1961) pp. 119–25.

4. R. S. Brumbaugh, "Applied Metaphysics: Truth and Passing Time," *Review of Metaphysics*, op. cit. In discussions of passage, propositions are given various definiteness values, V, ranging from 0 to 1. The point is, to allow for cases of partial correspondence between the future referent of a proposition and the proposition itself, where the future situation is only partially determinate as yet. One way of reading these values would be as truth-values in a Whiteheadian cosmos where there are three types of propositions, conformal, nonconformal, and partially conformal. But for my present purpose, the exact interpretation will not matter.

5. Primitive cultures may view seasonal and ritual cycles as numerically single; cp. Mircea Eliade, *The Myth of the Eternal Recurrence* trans. W. R. Trask, (New York: Pantheon Books, 1954). And cp. Aristotle, *De Generatione et Corruptione*, II.11, 337a35–338b20.

6. It casts some light on our knowledge of time to study the Platonic tradition's experiments with both of these senses of cyclic time as intermediate terms in a hierarchy connecting becoming with eternity.

7. In Aristotle's scheme, there is a radical break between the time of stars and the time we are immersed in, in our location in the less pure center of the cosmos. Aristotle, *Physics* II, 193a27: "That nature exists, it would be absurd to try to prove. . . ."

8. R. S. Brumbaugh, "Cosmography," *Review of Metaphysics*, 25, 1971, pp. 333–47; "Cosmography: The Problem of Modern Systems," *Review of Metaphysics*, 26, 1973, pp. 511–21; "Systems, Tenses, and Choices," *Midwestern Journal of Philosophy*, spring 1975, pp. 9–14.

9. A study of Plato's references to models of time discovers a set of four, which match the four levels of the divided line in the *Republic*; as the lower models are transcended by the higher, the set ends with a static metal mobile of the frozen harmonies of celestial motion. This is discussed in my "Plato and the History of Science," *Studium Generale*, 9, 1961, pp. 520–22.

10. There is a substantial literature treating biological time. A good introduction to the topic is given by the several articles on the theme in *Proceedings* I, II, and III.

11. Cp. Diotima's remarks on succession as the image of immortality in Plato's *Symposium* 206A1–B10.

12. My colleague in mathematics, Charles Rickart, has suggested that time measured by equal increments of growing older seems approximately related to calendar time as a logarithmic function.

13. E. M. Berkeley, "An Algebra of States and Events," *Scientific Monthly* 78 (1954), pp. 232–42. Later logical and computer work has more information and more elegance, but the states-events model of this article still seems to me exactly suited to describe subjective time.

14. This is the result of a U.S. Navy study of motion sickness: Christopher C. Sharp, "On the Dynamics of Motion Sickenss in a Seaway," *Scientific Monthly* 78 (1954) pp. 110–17.

15. I have already explored this difference in another discussion along with the other two subjective time senses of progressive and present eternal (the former recognizes *all* events, dividing at A, B, C, D, E, F; the latter recognizes *none*, so that there is a kind of single state quality here). I have been told that the Thematic Apperception Test in psychology is beginning to show a significant difference between perfective and inceptive responses, and a correlation of these with supposed "achievement."

16. H. Bergson, *Time and Free Will*, op. cit., pp. 191–98.

17. This is Bergson's point, made in his *Time and Free Will*, op. cit.

18. These linguistic roles certainly operate in the cases I can check at first hand, namely various Indo-European languages and literary Japanese. But my claim is that these or their equivalents are a practical necessity for *any* language. Historically, it seems that it is completion to which languages have paid most attention; but there are traces of other ways of setting up aspects and tenses. The primitive pessimism and fatalism of the world of the perfect tense is not the only one possible for an effective language system.

19. The new widespread use of digital watches and clocks gives an intuitive and practical content to this. In a discussion of D. Corish's paper, "Time, Space, and Freewill: The Leibniz-Clarke Correspondence" (*Proceedings* III, pp. 635–53), it was suggested that given free choice, Leibniz' God would be delighted by the new electronic watches with their fulgurant digits where Clarke's deity would insist on a railroadman's accurate conventional timepiece. This discussion, unfortunately, did not find its way into the *Proceedings* except for a tangential reference in my "Comments" on the paper, *Proceedings* III, pp. 656–57.

20. In a world of moments and states, there is another difference. Where the number series consists of actual terms that extend indefinitely in the "greater than" direction, the moment series consists of a set of actual terms which terminates at the present. All moments up to the present form an actual past-to-present series, but the future is not yet actual; so the series of actual moments always stops abruptly in the "t + " direction.

Chapter Seven

1. There is a general rule for the aesthetic relevance of musical vibration: simultaneous patterns with frequencies that are simple integral multiples are perceived as related by the category of the same, those that are not by that of the other. But otherness admits of many kinds, and the tones of a scale select, among these, intervals that are still integral but very complex in their lowest terms. A principle similar to this underlies the timekeeping regularity and interference patterns of waves of laser light.

Whitehead no doubt felt that the acoustical aspect of this relation justified his epigram: "music is mathematics overheard." On the other hand, the legendary 13th-century student expelled from the University of Paris for practicing the violin when he should have been "studying music," might be tempted to rejoin that pure mathematics is like a sequence of finger stops on inaudible strings, and without his violin it could never be heard or overheard.

2. For some years I have casually kept in mind a sort of inventory of items and experiences that I have found particularly aesthetically interesting. Surely this reflects my own idiosyncrasies and opportunities; but it could be that such collections of cases, compared, will add up to new principles, insights, vivid examples, or at worst subjects for general conversation. (Aristotle, after all, thought there should be a science of economics, with collections of anecdotes about the ways people had made money; and look at the science that has developed from this inception.)

Chapter Eight

1. In a recent legal case, a graduate sued an Eastern college because it had not carried out its promise to make him a liberally educated man; my sympathies are obviously with the plaintiff, though he was laughed out of court.

2. Cp. R. S. Brumbaugh, "Criticism in Philosophy: Aristotle's Literary Form," in B. Lang, ed., *Philosophical Style* (Chicago: Nelson Hall, 1980), pp. 294–310.

3. Jacob Klein, *A Commentary on Plato's Meno* (Chapel Hill: University of North Carolina Press, 1965); Richard Stanley H. Bluck, ed., *Plato's Meno* (Cambridge: Cambridge University Press, 1961); R. Sternfeld and Harold Zyskind, *Plato's Meno: A Philosophy of Man as Acquisitive* (Carbondale: Southern Illinois University Press, 1978). See also Malcom Brown, ed., *Plato's Meno: Text and Essays* (Indianapolis, Bobbs Merrill, 1971); and Brown's essay, "Plato Disapproves of the Slave-Boy's Answer," *Review of Metaphysics* 20 (1967), pp. 57–93.

4. Xenophon, *Anabasis* II.6, secs. 21–29.

5. Mary Helen Mayer, *The Philosophy of Teaching of St. Thomas Aquinas* (Milwaukee: The Bruce Publishing Company, 1929), has an English translation of the questions on teaching. She bases it on St. Thomas Aquinas, *Quaestiones Disputatae et Quaestiones Duodecim Quodlibetales* (5 vols., Rome, 1820) vol. 3: *De Veritate (1) Quaestion XI De Magistro (in Quatuor Articulos Divisa)*, pp. 273–76. The four questions are: (1) Whether man can teach and be called a teacher, or God alone? (2) Whether anyone can be called a teacher of himself? (3) Whether man may be taught by an angel? (4) Whether to teach is a function of the active or contemplative life?

6. " 'Even for many informed skeptics the question of the existence of extraterrestrial life has become not so much one of 'if' as of 'where'. . . for ultimate contact may be virtually inevitable,' said Dr. Richard Berendzen, provost of American University." "Scientists Ask Funding to Tune In on Universe," *New Haven Register*, September 20, 1978, p. 63, cols. 3–4.

7. See, for example, H. L. Dreyfuss, "Why Computers Must Have Bodies in Order to Be Intelligent," *Review of Metaphysics* 21 (1967), pp. 13–32.

8. Discussed in St. Thomas' resolution, Mayer, op. cit., pp. 74–76. See Wilder Penfield, *The Mystery of the Mind* (Princeton: Princeton University Press, 1975), foreword by Charles Hendel, pp. xvii–xxiv.

9. Response, Mayer, op. cit., p. 74: "About this mode of teaching by an angel we will not inquire because in this way [i.e., appearing sensibly and instructing with

audible words] an angel does not teach otherwise than a man does. . . ." But even here, the angel is superior; Reply to Objection 17, Mayer, p. 81.

10. Ibid., Response, par. 2, p. 74.

11. Ibid., Response, par. 3, p. 75.

12. Ibid.

13. Ibid., Reply to Objection 17, p. 81.

14. Ibid. For this defense, see particularly St. Thomas' Response to Question 1, par. 3, p. 50.

15. The psychology and epistemology of the Aristotelian tradition are technical and complex. For discussion, see, for example, Étienne H. Gilson, *La Philosophie au Moyen Age* (Paris: Payot, 1944) pp. 525–50; Richard P. McKeon, *Selections from Medieval Philosophers*, 2 vols. (New York: Scribners 1930) vol. 2, ix–xviii ("General Introduction"), pp. 149–234 ("St. Thomas Aquinas"), and pp. 422–515 ("Glossary").

16. Objection 17, Mayer, op. cit., p. 72.

17. Ibid., Reply to Objection 4, p. 76; also, Response, par. 3, p. 76.

18. Emanuel Swedenborg, *Heaven and Its Wonders and Hell*, trans. J. C. Ager (New York: Swedenborg Foundation 1950) pp. 121–25 (#162–169), pp. 141–45 (#191–199).

19. Reply to Objection 1, Mayer, op. cit., p. 76.

20. Ibid., Reply to Objection 11, p. 79.

21. Ibid., Reply to Objection 14: "The fact that something is spiritual does not prevent it from being suitable to act on something corporeal because nothing prevents the lower from being affected by the higher." The modern reader, with ideas of corporeality shaped by the 17th century, is not likely to accept this statement. And it may not be essential to the rest of the argument.

22. Ibid., Response, par. 2, p. 74; Reply to Objection 1, p. 76.

23. Ibid., Reply to Objection 17, p. 81. "Even in regard to those things which have causes determined in nature, an angel can teach more things than a man can, since an angel knows more things, and those things which an angel teaches, he teaches in a superior manner."

24. Ibid., Reply to Objection 12, p. 79.

25. Ibid., Reply to Objection 11, p. 79.

26. Ibid., Reply to Objection 10, p. 79.

27. Ibid., Reply to Objection 12, p. 79; Objection 12, pp. 70–71.

28. Ibid., Response, par. 1, p. 76.

29. Cp. ibid., Question 1, Response to Objection 18, p. 47; and Question 1, Response, par. 5, citing Aristotle, *Posterior Analytics*.

30. See ibid., Question 2, Response to Objection 4, p. 66.

31. See Henry Jackson, "Aristotle's Lecture Hall," *Journal of Philology* 35 (1920), p. 191 ff.

32. See n. 9 above.

33. I underscore emphatic because of its echo of St. Thomas' account of the way in which an angel gains our intellectual attention, Reply to Objection 2, Mayer, op cit., pp. 76–77.

34. A. N. Whitehead, *Introduction to Mathematics*, 12th impression (Oxford: Oxford University Press, 1948. Originally published Oxford, 1911) pp. 40–43.

35. Mayer, op. cit., in her commentary, p. 143, relates this shared illumination to the attitude of the teacher. "The last article [Question 2] emphasized the learner. The Third Article [Question 3] deals with the teacher, representing the human teacher as a

colleague on the faculty with God and the angels. The Second Article emphasized the necessity for scholarship [and, I would add, the radically non-reflexive character of 'instruction'], the Third Article brings out the inspirational value of a teacher's personality. . . ."

36. For example, television might offer a whole new range of possibilities for presenting sensations that could lead to new " . . . mixings of species in the phantasms of [the viewer's] imagination."

37. I am reminded here, just in passing, that Zen Buddhism favors two literary forms for teaching, the *koan* and the *mondo*. The *koan* is an arresting abstract paradox. The *mondo* is a concrete first-person biographical anecdote of education, sometimes retold in a perfective tense, but meant to be appreciated in the continuative present. (One of the most technically difficult, but most interesting, discussions of a phenomenologist's interpretation is an essay by Carlton Dallery, "On Being with Animals," in *On the Fifth Day*, ed. R. Morris and M. Fox. The least rewarding is B. F. Skinner's account of the future role of the live teacher as "entertainer," in *Beyond Freedom and Dignity*.)

Chapter Ten

1. Whitehead appeals to Aristotle's doctrine of the Prime Mover as one of the last discussions of the existence of God by an impartial metaphysician (*Science and the Modern World*, Chap. XII). He might well have followed this discussion by quoting *Metaphysics* Lambda viii, Aristotle's appraisal of later established religions and their contrast to an earlier pure religious vision.

> There is a very ancient tradition in the form of a myth, that the stars are gods and that the divine embraces the whole of nature. The remaining features of popular religion were added at a later date in order to frighten ignorant people, to lend sanction to the laws, and on general utilitarian grounds: these gods are said to be in the form of men or beasts, and other stories of that kind are told. But if we strip the original doctrine of its later accretions, and consider it alone, we cannot but recognize it as inspired. It teaches that the prime substances are gods, and is a relic of that perfect flowering of the arts and sciences which must have been often achieved and often lost. It is, so to speak, the surviving relic of an ancient treasure, allowing us a fleeting glimpse of what our early ancestors believed.
>
> *Metaphysics* Lambda viii,
> trans. John Warrington,
> New York, E.P. Dutton,
> 1956 (Everyman's Library, p. 357).

2. Here I follow Whitehead's analysis of "Interest" and "Importance" in *The Function of Reason* (Princeton: Princeton University Press, 1929). This gives a philosophical account that does not presuppose "non-classical theology."

Index